WESTLIFE

Years

WESTLIFE

OUR STORY

WITH MARTIN ROACH

HarperCollins*Publishers*

HarperCollins *Publishers*
77–85 Fulham Palace Road,
Hammersmith, London W6 8JB

First published 2008

2

© Westlife 2008

Westlife asserts the moral right to be
identified as the author of this work

A catalogue record of this book is
available from the British Library

HB ISBN-13 978-0-00-728812-0
HB ISBN-10 0-00-728812-3
PB ISBN-13 978-0-00-728813-7
PB ISBN-10 0-00-728813-1

Printed and bound in Great Britain by
Clays Ltd, St Ives plc

Parental advisory
This book contains strong language
and may not be suitable for children.

Mixed Sources
Product group from well-managed
forests and other controlled sources
www.fsc.org Cert no. SW-COC-1806
© 1996 Forest Stewardship Council
FSC

We dedicate this book to our parents

ACKNOWLEDGEMENTS

Would be impossible to thank everyone who has been in our lives over the past ten years, but to all who have been there and supported us – thank you!

To our manager and friend, Louis Walsh

CONTENTS

PART II

PART III

PROLOGUE

'So, Westlife, what do you think of Brazil?'

We were sitting on the top of a shaking tour bus, being interviewed by a well-known DJ in Rio de Janeiro, live on radio.

Around the tour bus were 3,000 Westlife fans, all screaming and chanting.

Back home, we'd already seen our first seven singles go straight in at number 1, a feat no band before us had ever achieved. We'd sold millions of albums around the world and gone from being unknowns in an aspiring boy band from Ireland to the front of every pop magazine in the world in just over a year.

Westlife was a phenomenon, without a doubt.

We'd been due at that Rio radio station, but there'd been so many fans waiting for us outside that we were unable to get anywhere near and our personal safety would have been at risk – had we tried to get off the bus we'd have been pulled apart.

As we'd pulled around the corner, the screaming crowd had surrounded the vehicle in a heartbeat and started banging on the sides, rocking the bus, chanting and screaming. It was mental. Several of us actually pushed our backs and shoulders up against the glass because we thought the windows were going to cave in.

We were loving it.

We got our cameras and handycams out and were filming the fans as they were filming us. It was great.

The security men made us climb up through one of the bus skylights onto the roof and do the interview there.

There seemed only one thing we could say in reply to the DJ's question: *'We love Brazil!'*

The screaming was so loud we thought our eardrums were going to burst.

It is a long way home to the gentle pace of rural Ireland, Sligo and suburban Dublin from Rio de Janeiro, but the journey to the roof of that bus – and beyond – would see a lot more twists and turns than any of us could ever have imagined.

Here's how we did it.

Part I

CHAPTER ONE

TOWN OF PLENTY

For 35 years, my parents, Mae and Peter Filan, ran the Carlton café right in the middle of Sligo, on the west coast of Ireland. The whole family – all nine of us – lived in the house above it. We loved living there.

I was born on 5 July 1979, Shane Steven Filan, the youngest of seven children. God knows how my parents looked after all of us. As well as myself, there were my sisters Yvonne, Denise and Mairead, and my brothers Finbarr, Peter and Liam. Dad was the cook and Mam ran the restaurant. They worked very hard and we didn't go without a thing. We weren't rich, don't be getting me wrong, but if we needed something, they managed to get the money together to buy it. There was always a few quid there.

That house above the café gives me my very earliest memory. When I was three, I burnt my hand on the cooker in our kitchen. I remember as if it was yesterday reaching up to put my hand on the ring, then roaring and crying when it burnt me. I can still see the dog outside the room looking in at all the commotion. Mam calmed me down and put cold milk on the burn to soothe the pain. It's a strong, vivid, first memory.

I loved having so many brothers and sisters around. My parents had had four kids back to back, with only a year between each. Then three more children followed with a two-year gap between each. My mum had her last baby, me, when she was 42. For some reason she'd always wanted seven kids and I think she just kept going till she got them. Back then it was very common to have at least four kids, to have just two kids wasn't the norm. There were a lot more big families then than there are now, certainly in the west of Ireland anyway.

I never got picked on because I had those older brothers, so that made my life a lot easier than some. Maybe I got a little spoiled occasionally, as the youngest, but to be honest because there were seven of us Mam and Dad didn't have time to spoil us, they were so busy just looking after us and feeding us and all that. It was a good life.

What we did have was a lot of chips! Perhaps I'm remembering wrong, but it seemed like we had chips five or six nights a week. No wonder really – now I've got my own family I've learned how much looking after kids costs, so perhaps it was cheap and easy. Chips and cans of Fanta and Coke – whenever I see those it reminds me of my childhood. I loved it; the café was busy and there was always something happening and interesting people coming in.

After that, my mind flits to the first day at Fatima Primary School, when I was four. It was run by nuns and I was gripped by sheer bloody fear. I stood in line at the entrance, waiting to enrol, holding on to my mum's hand very tightly. One of the kids ran out of line and a nun went over to him, shouted something and then smacked him on the bum.

'These nuns don't look too happy, Mam,' I said.

Mam just laughed and said not to worry.

A few days later, I'd started to settle in but was still a little anxious. One of my brothers was in the school across the road and one afternoon I noticed he'd put his nose against the window and was pulling faces and waving at me. I just burst out crying, bawled my eyes out, I did. That was all just early nerves, though. In fact it was a great school.

I'd already started singing when I went to primary. Funnily enough, 'Uptown Girl' by Billy Joel was my party piece. I'd be wheeled out at family dos; my mum used to make me get up in front of all the aunties and uncles to sing that song. Pure embarrassment, like. So I was rehearsing for the Westlife version way back then!

There was no musical background in my family, however. My dad's a good singer and Yvonne, my sister, could sing all the hymns well at church, but there was no real background of singing or music there. Growing up, my big thing was Michael Jackson. I was a mental Michael Jackson fan, *mental*. The *Bad* album was on constantly in our house – 'Man in the Mirror', all those songs. That and *Thriller*. Jesus, I just wanted to be a star, a famous singer, up on stage. I'd sing all Jackson's tunes in the mirror or in front of my sisters, but I was afraid of singing in front of a crowd. At that early point I was just taking Michael Jackson off really, copying him. I used to be quite good at mimicking people. Gradually, I developed my own style and my own voice and felt more confident about singing in front of people, but I never had the courage to go on stage until I was 12.

In class, I was an OK student, usually a C+, the occasional B, nothing spectacularly good or bad. My attention drifted very easily. There wasn't really any subject I loved. I wasn't academic and I didn't have any dreams to become a doctor or a lawyer. I enjoyed the craic with the lads, I was in a decent class and there weren't really any eejits in the group, so we all had a laugh. Apart from that, I never really enjoyed school that much, to be honest with you, it was just OK.

The most exciting thing about school was what happened afterwards. I was always talking and trying to sort out something to do after class: 'Where are we going? What are we doing?' I played rugby a bit and some Gaelic football, but all I really wanted to do was sing. There was no class for that, so for me it was like, *OK, I'm going to do this school thing because I have to, but really I want to be in a band.*

Then I started auditioning for musicals at school. Those auditions, rehearsals and performances are my fondest memories of my time at school. It was an all-boys school, so the girls would come up from their school and we'd all stay late for maybe three hours, working through rehearsals. It only happened for about six weeks of each school year, but it meant everything to me, my whole life revolved around it.

The first big break I got was at the Hawks Well Theatre in an adult production of *Grease*. It was put on by a woman called Mary McDonagh. She was the choreographer, director and producer, and was a pretty well-known name in Sligo. She brought a lot of people up through the ranks in the theatre, offering them their first roles and giving them confidence on stage. She was a great director. She gave me the role of Danny Zuko's younger brother in this version of

Grease. Also in the cast was a kid a year younger than me who I'd seen around town. His name was Kian Egan.

*   *   *

'Mum, can we go to the *feis* now, please?'

'Alright, Kian, come on, but we'll have to be quick.'

I was sitting in the doctor's waiting room, having just been seen about an ear infection. I was anxious to get out because my mum had entered me in a local poetry competition, called a *feis*. I was only four, but this was quite a big thing in Ireland, especially in Easter week. They'd hold a *feis* and you'd go on stage and recite a poem. Sometimes there'd be over 100 kids competing. However, I'd been quite ill with this ear infection so I actually missed my slot because Mum had been worried and had taken me to the doctor's. When we finally got to the competition, though, she persuaded the poetry judges to give me a later slot.

I won.

My mum and dad, Kevin and Patricia Egan, were like that – always encouraging their kids. I come from a big family of four brothers and three sisters – Viveanne, Gavin, Fenella and Tom, who are older, and Marielle and Colm, who are younger. Dad met my mum at the dance, they became dance partners and eventually started going out with each other. The first baby arrived when they were only 20; I arrived on 29 April 1980.

My dad was an electrician for the Electricity Supply Board of Ireland, so he'd be out all hours sending the young fellas climbing up the poles, organizing all that. His family didn't have anything, so he'd had to go to work at 16. Mum was a housewife. She had seven kids to look after, so she didn't have a spare minute.

My dad had been brought up in Leitrim, a very rural area. His childhood was very typical of the west coast of Ireland at that point, then he set up the family home in nearby Sligo. It was a very busy home. At one point there would have been seven or eight of us in the house, all squeezing into bunk-beds and stuff like that. We weren't rich, but it was fine. I have a lot of great memories of my childhood and we remain a very tight family to this day.

My mum wasn't musical at all. I used to sit her at the piano to teach her 'Baa, Baa, Black Sheep', but she couldn't get it. My dad, on the other hand, would have had it in five minutes. He never played an instrument, though. When he was younger, the opportunity wasn't necessarily there – if he'd said he wanted to be in a band, it would have been, 'Away with you, get back to work.' In his later years, however, I realized how much of a love for music he had and became more aware of his massive record collection.

All of us kids tried our hand at music. My eldest brother is, in my eyes, a piano genius – he's the vice principal of a school in Sheffield now, with honours degrees in piano and guitar. As a kid, he was a classical whizz on piano, so he started teaching me piano at a young age. Every single member of my family before me learned the piano and my other brother started playing trombone in a concert band and then bass in his own rock band.

I did the poetry competitions every year from the age of four and would end up with five or six first places each year. My mother would teach me the poems in the kitchen. I would always be in the prizes, and also started winning story telling competitions too. I was quite confident as a kid in that sense. But it was my mum who did it really – she put her all into it, and there's no doubt about it, I wouldn't be doing Westlife now if it wasn't for my mother.

Most amazingly, she did it for all of us, not just me. Even though she had seven kids, she had the drive to get us out of bed every Saturday morning for speech and drama lessons, or out for piano lessons every Tuesday night, or guitar lessons on a Wednesday night or football on a Thursday. She still does it with my younger brother to this day. She's done it with all seven of us.

Then one of my sisters started to do variety musicals at the community hall. Along with Mum, she'd put a show together with singing, acting, comedy, all sorts of stuff. I was the guitar player and the singer and the comedian and the guy who dressed up as a woman and all that type of stuff. My first cousin Gillian, who later married Shane, was also in that.

I loved all this because I was what I call an 'out of school' kid. That's where I was happiest, not in class. The teachers absolutely hated me because I was too giddy in class; unless I liked the subject I was as giddy as shit.

I did the poetry competitions right up until I was 16, but by then I had discovered rock music and lost interest in reciting poetry, to be honest with you. One of my elder brothers had a rock band and I started listening to stuff like Metallica, Guns N'Roses, Bon Jovi, Green Day, Pearl Jam, rock and metal bands. Albums like *Dookie* I just played constantly and, like millions of other kids, I sat in my bedroom for hours trying to learn 'Seek & Destroy' and loads of other Metallica songs.

My dad had somehow managed to buy me an electric guitar by this stage. I'd badgered him for a year to get it, then one day my sister arrived back from college with a surprise package for me, a black guitar – an Aria Pro 2, NA20B. I recall the exact model number. It cost £300, which for a guitar was ludicrous. Of course, being a teenager, then I was after an amplifier: 'You have to have an amp to go with it!' I hounded Dad until he bought me a second-hand Orange amp, which is one of the most classic pieces of amplification you can buy. I didn't know this at the time – I just knew if I plugged my guitar in, smacked the distortion pedal on to ten and switched it to maximum volume, it sounded amazing.

Inevitably, I started forming my own bands. During my school years, there were loads of different bands and line-ups, most famously Skrod, an Irish word for which the closest translation is a woman's private parts. After that, we became Pyromania and began a fierce rivalry with my older brother's rock band, Bert and the Cookie Monsters. Hardly Oasis versus Blur, but it mattered so much to us at the time! We would go around the school ripping down their posters and they would do the same to ours. They nearly always won any battle of the bands because they were older, but we thought we were the best.

At one memorable band night at Summerhill College, I brought out the best-looking teacher in front of a hall crammed with students, serenaded her with 'Wonderful Tonight' by Eric Clapton and then gave her a peck on the cheek. I was the king for weeks off the back of that.

I was in and out of various line-ups; it all changed so many times. We'd practise in people's living rooms, including two friends called Michael Walsh and Derek 'Buff' Gannon. The eldest brother of my cousin Gillian had a band called, rather fantastically, Repulse, a thrash metal outfit. One time they got on a Saturday morning TV show, God knows how, and we were all so excited we went along to support them. You can see me in the background with my long, dark hair, head banging to Repulse.

I'd started to get quite good at the guitar, but one day I completely scuppered my chances of being in the next Metallica. Our drummer at the time was out on his bike with me and we were at the top of a hill. He said, 'Jump on, Kian, I'll take you down the hill.' So, being 15 and all that, I jumped onto his handlebars and we flew down this hill.

At the bottom of the hill there was a sharp right turn and a wall.

We were going way too fast.

He didn't make the turn.

I slammed into the wall face first.

I've still got the scar to show for it, on my right cheek. Worse still, though, I'd broken my finger, in fact the bone was actually sticking out, completely dislocated. I was in agony and an ambulance was called. I had to have three operations and to cut a long story short – or rather to cut a long digit short – the finger stopped growing. So now it's shorter than my other fingers and crooked.

Which isn't the best news if you want to be the next James Hetfield.

More immediately, our most recent variety show had got through to the All Ireland finals and I was one of the guitar players. I only had two weeks to learn how to play my part with two fingers bandaged up. I could still play, but it had to be mostly bar chords. That accident pretty much finished any guitar prospects I might have had.

If you'd have been at school with me, you may well have thought I was a cocky little shit. Certainly the older boys did and it caused me a lot of grief. If I saw someone picking a fight with my brother

Tom, for example, even though he could look after himself I'd run over and try to stand up for him. 'Get off my brother!' I'd shout, which always embarrassed him because, of course, I was his little brother.

Unfortunately, I got hit plenty. There were some rough times back then. At times it was ridiculous and, to be totally honest with you, I still carry a lot of anger about those years with me now. There were some dark days.

The thing was, I suppose I had a bit of a name for myself. I was well known and popular with the girls from all different parts of the town. It was just kids playing at relationships, but the guys from the same area as these girls didn't like it at all. As a result, I got bullied quite a bit by the older, tougher guys. I'm a little reluctant to call it bullying, it was and it wasn't. It started off with verbal abuse, but soon escalated to actual physical violence. I recall walking home from one carnival with a split lip and getting hit at a school disco. One time I was walking along the street when three boys came across to me and – BAM! BAM! BAM! – they all punched me for no reason.

I've had too many black eyes, although luckily I never got a broken nose, even though plenty tried to give me one. The west coast of Ireland is full of very tough people. I don't mean bullies, I mean people who have had a hard, difficult life. So these sort of fights were commonplace and, to be honest, unless you were put in hospital, it wasn't a big deal.

It got worse, though. One day I was at home and the doorbell rang. I got up, opened the door and BAM, this guy standing there just punched me in the face. My mum was horrified and called the police, but nothing came of it.

It eventually got to the stage where I couldn't go into town, particularly on a weekend, because I knew there were a handful of guys – young men, really, by this stage – who were after me.

At this point, I never hit back. I thought that if I hit them back, I was going to have ten of them on my doorstep the next night. And I would have, no doubt about it.

It's improved enormously now, but like many towns, Sligo was rough in many areas when I was growing up and I couldn't go to most places without some bother. It affected me massively for some time and I begged my mum to send me to music boarding school, because I just wanted to get out of town so badly. My eldest brother Gavin had told me about these schools where they organized rock bands and all that, and they sounded great, but the main reason I wanted to go to boarding school was to get out of Sligo. Of course there was no way my parents could afford that, so I had to live with the situation on the streets. I started lifting weights and got quite good quite quickly – not to compete with these people, but just to give myself some confidence.

Then one day, when I'd reached 16, I hit back.

I was with my cousin Gillian that day, just walking around town down by the supermarket. She used to introduce me to a few of the birds she knew and it was normally great craic. But not that time.

A few days before, I'd been at a Sligo Rovers football match and some kid had come up to me and said, 'Watch out, so-and-so is after you 'cos he heard you called his mum a whore.' He was talking about the local hard knock. I just knew this little shit would later say to that same hard knock, 'I saw Kian Egan at the football match and he called your mother a whore.'

Anyway, we were in the arcade and I noticed this hard knock and five of his mates across the way. They were all staring at me.

'Gillian, let's go. Come on.'

'Why?'

'That's yer man who is after me.'

'Why don't you just go up to him and say something?' Gillian didn't stand for no messing.

'No, no, come on, let's just go.'

I grabbed her arm and we walked out of the arcade, but I could sense immediately that they were following us. By the time we'd walked down the street and round the corner, they'd caught up with us.

I was shitting myself.

'Egan! Egan! Did you call my mother a whore?'

'No, I did not. I don't even know who you are, I've never seen you before in my life.' Then I said, 'My mum is waiting for me to go and pick some shoes.'

No good.

'Meet me in the car park in 15 minutes. We'll sort this out,' he said.

This was ridiculous.

'Look, if you want to hit me, do it now. I don't want to wait 15 minutes, just do it now.'

I'm not gonna pretend – I was absolutely shitting my pants. I was terrified.

He took a swing and I reacted, finally. I blocked him and then hit back ... *hard*. I just laid into him and really let loose. It was three years of frustration coming out. He'd picked on me on the wrong day.

But I wasn't out of the woods yet. Word spread that I would hit back and some of these idiots saw that as a challenge. So when I got a little older, going to nightclubs and getting well pissed was always a bit risky. I often went out with my friend Graham, who would later join me at the start of the Westlife tale, and he was a hard lad, very capable of looking after himself. He had a bit of a reputation because he was from a slightly rougher part of town. If I was with him, people would leave me alone – he used to say, 'If you hit him, I'll hit you!' However, if I went out alone or without Graham, it could get very nasty. Many times I would arrive at a club, spot a few faces in the crowd and just do a U-turn and leave.

Sometimes, however, confrontation was unavoidable, but even then I tried my best not to hit back unless I absolutely had to. Generally, I would let someone hit me three times before striking back. I figured if they hit me more than three times, I had to do something to defend myself. I would always say, 'I don't want to fight you, let's leave it,' but sometimes I was in a corner.

Since I'm being very open here, I must say that I was never going to move onto the next level: physically abusing people. I didn't want to punch anybody, I was never a fighter, I only ever hit someone because I had no choice, you know, I was defending myself. Just sitting talking about the shit I let myself go through with these guys is annoying, it makes me angry. Kids shouldn't have to deal with all that.

I know I have the benefit of hindsight now, but I think those difficult times made me a much stronger person today. I think they taught me a hell of a lot about life at a young age and helped me to be the person I am.

Since Westlife has become successful, one or two of these guys have come up to me in Sligo, apologized for their behaviour and offered to buy me a pint. I haven't taken the pints, but it's interesting to see the change.

I am being brutally honest with you when I say that I did sometimes turn on those who were smaller than me. I never hit anyone, but I did call people names. It made me feel better, albeit momentarily, I'm afraid to say. I was stuck in the middle between the older, tougher boys who would kick the living daylights out of you and the quieter guys, often from the country, who came into school. It was a strange cruel pecking order. One day we pushed a kid into the shower with his brand new tracksuit and trainers on. His name was Mark Feehily.

To You, Our Fan,
Reading this...

this year is very special
because it is celebrating
10 Years of Westlife
It has been the best
10 years of my life and
you have been a massive
part of it, for that
thankyou so much!

Love Always
Shane

MARK xx   Kian   Shane   Nicky

CHAPTER TWO

WARM EVENINGS, CRISP MORNINGS, EARLY BEGINNINGS

My Feehily family home was a four-bedroomed bungalow in the countryside near Sligo. It was a rural upbringing and I loved every minute of it.

Both my parents, Oliver and Marie Feehily, worked. Mum was a civil servant in the Department of Agriculture; Dad worked in the building trade. She worked nine to five, but once she clocked out of that job, she clocked into motherhood and providing a taxi service for her kids. I was born Mark Patrick Michael Feehily on 28 May 1980, followed by my younger brothers Barry and Colin. We just lived too far out of town to walk or cycle in every day, so Mum used to drive us around constantly.

I spent a lot time at my granny's house when both my parents were out at work. She lived in a cottage on a big farm in acres of idyllic Irish countryside. That was even more remote than my home, but I loved it and loads of my cousins used to go round there too. It was brilliant. My dad's mum is just the most loving woman in the world.

My mum's mum lived on the other side of Sligo, so we saw her on a Sunday usually. Granddad was the landlord of a famous pub in Sligo town, which is where my mum grew up. Everyone knew him, so if I said I was Paddy Verdon's grandson, they'd know who I was straight away. Verdon's Bar on the Mall was very well known and Granddad was a big personality, he loved his grandkids very much. He was just this loving character full of stories – we would listen to him absolutely glued. He once told us that he had about 50 stallions kept on a mountain top. They were beautiful stories that he'd tell. He was extremely handy, too; he used to make furniture, all sorts. He had all the modern things too – TVs, videos. I remember he had a hi-fi that was way ahead of its time and I recall blasting *The Bodyguard* soundtrack out of it! Nana was lovely too. She was an amazing cook and every Sunday we'd eat this amazing home-baked brown bread with cheese, and ham sandwiches. Both sets of grandparents were very positive, incredibly loving aspects of my childhood. They were like an extension of my parents.

At my own home, when Mum and Dad came back from work we'd all congregate in the kitchen or living room and the telly would be blasting out, people would be doing homework or playing and there'd be loads of chatting – it was never a case of everyone going to their own rooms. It was a very close-knit, exciting, loving family.

I spent my youth walking in triangles. One point was our bungalow, another point was my granny's house and the third point was school. And that little triangle was surrounded by fields and farms. That was my world. It's funny now, because I might hop on a plane to Los Angeles with the band or for a holiday and not bat an eyelid, but back then a trip into Sligo on a Saturday was a major treat.

Since we've become well known, a lot of attention has been given to Sligo. Some journalists like to make out it's a very rural small-time town in the west of Ireland. That's just a cliché. It isn't. Some people did stay there and work the same jobs as their parents, yes, but loads of others went off and found fantastic new careers elsewhere. It had a good mixture of shops and plenty of culture – pubs and clubs where they played all kinds of music. It was – and still is – a place where the arts literally thrive, especially music.There are lots of artists and singers. Michael Flatley's dad comes from Sligo, W. B. Yeats spent much of his childhood and wrote poetry there and Spike Milligan lived there in Holborn Street. Sligo has an awful lot of culture and history; it's a lovely place.

Back as a kid, though, my first access to music was at my granny's house and also through my dad's record collection. The west of Ireland has got a culture of country music. Up in Donegal they've got quite famous country singers, people like Sandy Kelly. The local radio played a mixture of American country and Irish country, and my granny loved listening to those stations.

My dad had the weirdest, most interesting record collection. I don't know how he accumulated such an odd mix. He had Queen, *Top of the Pops* compilations, Eddy Grant albums, Nana Mouskouri, Gladys Knight and the Pips, the *Jesus Christ Superstar* soundtrack, all sorts. For some reason he used to put his record player out in the garage and I'd go in there and hear all this eclectic stuff.

It was a slower way of life than in the town. When you're a child living in the countryside, you can spend hours doing things and you don't even realize how the time has passed by.

My primary school, St Patrick's, was beautiful and I loved it. On the very first day I was very apprehensive because I didn't like strangers or kids I didn't know. But once I got into it, I loved it. It was out in the countryside, bathed in fresh air. I was very lucky. I was a very peaceful kind of child and that school was a very peaceful place to go every day.

Then one day my dad came home with this enormous satellite dish. He had been working on a house and they had wanted to throw this thing away, so he had brought it home. Suddenly, instead of, like, four channels, we had 400. I could get tons of American music channels – early hip-hop, music television, loads of stuff. That had a huge impact on me. Funnily enough, we got a microwave around the same time – we were one of the first families I knew to get one – so that, along with my satellite dish and a new pair of trainers I'd just got, made me feel like I was the richest kid on Earth. We weren't rich at all, though. My dad had just got lucky with this random old satellite.

There was a lot of music at school, which is typical of Irish education. All my schools taught tin whistle in class, for example. And we'd sing; nearly every day we used to sing. So I was brought up around this very random collection of all sorts of music from different cultures, different countries – a real mixture.

The common denominator in all of this was the singing – I *loved* to sing. If it was an Irish country classic, I'd sing it; if it was an R&B or hip-hop tune, I'd sing the chorus melody in between the rap verses; if it was an American pop tune I'd heard on satellite, I'd sing that.

Then I discovered Mariah Carey and Whitney Houston. I must have shattered my parents' eardrums singing along to 'I Will Always Love You'. Mariah was my favourite, though, and when I first heard 'Hero' it had a huge impact on me. My dad saw her on the telly and called up to my bedroom for me to go down. I did and just stood there in silence and watched the whole song. I'd never seen or heard of her before and I was very drawn to her gospel voice and beautiful image. I just remember looking at her and thinking how absolutely gorgeous she was, and then she sang and her voice was out of this world. Hearing her sing was a rare moment for me, because that was the awakening of my love for pop music. I literally think at that precise second listening to that song something awakened in me, without a shadow of a doubt. If I hadn't seen her that day, maybe the door to music and eventually Westlife wouldn't have opened. Who knows? But after that I started rooting out soul and gospel tunes and completely immersed myself in music. I also started singing a lot at school. At first I was crap, singing way too loud, and it drove the teachers insane. I would belt out 'Silent Night' or the latest pop song at full blast. But I started to improve and I couldn't stop myself, I just loved singing.

Inevitably, I starting singing in school plays and productions. The first thing I did was a play called *Scrooged* and I just absolutely got a major buzz from it, on this tiny little stage. I was only about eight but I loved it. I was extremely self-conscious as a kid – something I still carry with me to this day to a certain extent – but I noticed that when I sang, all the anxiety fell away, I didn't care who was singing with me or listening to me, as long as I was singing I was happy.

It was the same at Mass. We weren't an overly religious family, but we did go to Mass and I really enjoyed the singing there. The first time I sang in front of people was at church – 'Away in a Manger', on Christmas Eve at midnight Mass. The acoustics were so amazing. It wasn't a huge church, but it had a lovely echo, and the smell of incense is still with me today. I just really enjoyed it and

I didn't care for one second that people were watching me. Each week, there might be a couple of teachers and some older boys in the choir – had that been a room full of people chatting, I wouldn't have said a word. But as it was singing, I had no self-doubt and no awkwardness at all. During that time I realized that gospel affected me more deeply than any other music. It still has a power over me. It is something special, unique.

I think I was quite well behaved as a kid, but I'm not going to say I was very, very obedient. Occasionally I used to kick up a stink with my parents, but all kids do at some point. Mum and Dad said I had to be responsible for my own homework and I did it. I was allowed to do it when I wanted to, as long as I got it done. That was reflective of their attitude generally: they respected the kids and gave them the space to grow up and be themselves. And I just wanted to give back a bit of the love my parents and grandparents showed me.

One of the first big moments on stage for me was a talent competition at school in front of the whole hall. It was maybe a few hundred kids, but it felt like a few thousand. It was the same night Kian serenaded the teacher with 'Wonderful Tonight'. There were two other lads in the talent competition that were my age; one did line dancing and one sang a Garth Brookes song. Both got booed. I won my category and age group and I didn't get booed, I didn't get laughed at, I got clapped. People weren't bouncing off the ceiling, but I got clapped. That was a key moment for me.

Outside of when I was singing, I was a pretty introspective child at school. I was quiet, reserved, nervous. That was how I was all the time – except when I was singing. It's strange. I don't know why it was, but I didn't question it, I just enjoyed it. Even today, singing is the one thing I can do and not feel embarrassed. I just get into the zone and start singing and lose myself.

When I went to the secondary school at Summerhill College in Sligo, I had to get used to a less idyllic routine than at the primary. The boys from town were tougher and, being very honest with you, I did get some stick. For a long time, it mattered to me what people thought of me. If someone put pen on my cheek or if I had dog shit on my shoe, like kids do, I would be so embarrassed. Stuff like that made me want to crawl up into a ball. If anyone ever pointed at me and laughed, I was gutted. If I played tennis and someone said I was rubbish, it would break my heart. I was only a kid, 12 years old or so, but I just wasn't that hard and stuff like that made a deep impression on me. I sort of wish I wasn't like that, because life would have been a lot easier if I didn't give a shit, like some people.

*　　*　　*

We thought pushing Mark into the shower was just a bit of fun, *explains Kian*, but it wasn't to him. The name-calling was hurtful. I'm very glad to say that despite this we very quickly became good friends, hanging around with each other, great mates.

Mark had a difficult time with certain people. A little bit because of his weight, but also because he was a singer, he was quiet, he was from the country – you know, he did different things from everyone else. I was a good sports player, I was good at Gaelic football; when I was 17, I played in the All Ireland quarter finals, and that sportiness always helps a kid at school. Even then, the rougher edges of my childhood sometimes spilled over into my sports. In that All Ireland game, two great big buffs from the country ran full pelt and sandwiched me. These guys must have been up at six lifting hay bales and spent all day eating potatoes and cabbage. Jesus, it hurt. I got straight up and headbutted the pair of them. Well, that was that – banned for three months.

Mark was in my class and I started hanging round with him when I was 14. By then I'd progressed from my sister's variety shows to musicals at the school and the local theatre. That's when I started hanging out with Shane, who was a year older than me – during break-time and through rehearsing these musicals. You might not think that getting into musicals was particularly a good idea for someone like me, with all the situations I got from the Sligo hard knocks. But do you know what? We made it look *good*!

The Hawks Well Theatre plays a big part in my story and that of Westlife, *explains Mark*. I had front-row tickets to a production of *Grease* – my first musical – with my mum, her sister and her kids. These cousins, the Normans, were all really talented actresses, so they loved going to the theatre. This first time I went along I was so excited, and as soon as I saw the stage itself, I wanted to be on it.

Then the musical started and out walked this tiny fucking pip-squeak followed by a slightly less tiny but greasier bastard with long grungy hair. It was Shane and Kian.

They were the T-Birds and I couldn't believe how good they were. I was mesmerized by Shane's voice. He sang 'We Go Together' and it was incredible. I actually knew of him from school. He had a floppy haircut and all the girls fancied him. We weren't close mates, yet somehow that made it all the more amazing – this kid from school who could sing like this. Even back in the day, he had that perfect voice. The dance moves were also perfectly done. He was a natural. I was blown away, basically. When I saw Shane out there on the stage, for me that was the start of Westlife.

Kian was the rock child, the grungy one with the long hair, the edge. He had long brown hair all over his face, even though he was in *Grease*. But he had a real presence, a real charm about him. The girls all fancied him too. The two of them were brilliant and that night, *that* performance, made me want to be on stage for life.

There were only really two little parts in *Grease* for me and Kian, *says Shane*. Mary had pretty much made the roles for us. She knew we had talent and that we were up for a challenge. As I said, I was Danny Zuko's younger brother, and she put us two on stage for this one little song. On the first night, I was very nervous, but after that it was just like, *Oh my God, I love this!* We came on and it was all very cute. You could see people thinking, *Ah, look at the two little lads.* But we were deadly serious. That was my first big moment on stage and I remember absolutely loving it. There were 400 people there and, for me, this was the big time.

After seeing Shane and Kian in *Grease*, I was desperate to get my own first role, *continues Mark*. There was a classifieds section in the local paper called 'Bits and Pieces' that listed anything from 'Happy 40th Birthday, Kaye, from the boys,' to notices of weddings and adverts for auditions. I would literally scan this section every week, all excited, hoping to find something I could audition for. That shows how little I knew about the business – getting a part in one of these musicals seemed so distant, so impossible. Yet, looking back, all I needed to do was walk into the foyer of the theatre, find out the director and ask for a part.

I never had any formal training, I just learned by listening and singing. It was just a pure, bare love of singing. My parents didn't push me and they didn't pull me back, either. They just catered for the fact that I was banging on about singing 24/7 – talked about it and lived it and breathed it even back then. I was infatuated by it. I do have a tendency to latch on to things in life, especially if I find something that I love or someone who perhaps can say things I'm struggling to articulate, and that's what singing did for me.

The first real musical opportunity was the school production of *Annie Get your Gun*. I went to the auditions for that and sang a few tunes, and the teacher just nodded and said, 'Fine, Feehily, you're in.'

Simple as that.

He had to get through like 200 students, but he probably had an inkling I had a bit of a voice – or maybe he was only doing it to keep out the people who were really, really bad. But I felt like I was being offered a place in some big drama school or something. It felt like a huge step up.

Shane was in the same musical, playing a woman called Jessie. So was Kian. Because it was an all-boys school, you had all these burly Irish teenagers in drag.

Initially, I was too shy to go up and talk to him. Shane and Kian were quite cool at school. Shane was popular with the guys and the girls. Kian used to get in a bit of trouble with the guys because all their girlfriends fancied him, while Shane somehow managed to be cool with the guys and the girls. Eventually I plucked up the courage to speak to him.

I'd seen Mark in a couple of talent shows and I knew he was amazing, *remembers Shane.* He more or less had a black person's soul voice, like. He had this R&B soulful tone. He stood out like a sore thumb.

We quickly realized how much we both liked singing, *continues Mark,* and I think we respected each other as a result. We started hanging out away from school. We'd often go down town to get a takeaway and share a large curry with, like, ten people. Then one day Shane said, 'Why don't you come over to my house on Saturday?' and we started forming a friendship between just the two of us.

I started doing musicals, some with Shane and some without. I really enjoyed the camaraderie backstage and the way everyone knew each other. Living in the country like I did, I used to spend a fair bit of time by myself – not so much when I got home, but on the long walk back from school down the lanes, thinking. The musicals were brilliant because they were so lively and there always someone who would stay behind after the show or go out. You never had to be by yourself. I used to love that element of it. Everyone was friends with everyone, it was an amazingly pure and enjoyable atmosphere.

Plus, when you performed, no one was reviewing you or criticizing you. It was a small town musical and everyone wanted it to be perfect, but at the same time you weren't being scrutinized. Even when they handed out the lead roles, people who'd hoped to get that part but hadn't weren't bitchy or nasty, they were pleased for the other person. There was a certain innocence to it, it was all purely for fun and enjoyment, and we always seemed to get applauded.

I was the lead a few times, though I wasn't so good when it came to acting. In fact I used to curl up and die when I had to act – still do, sometimes, when I'm on telly. But if it was singing, I loved it.

My biggest role so far, *explains Shane*, came as the Artful Dodger in *Oliver Twist*, another school production. The Dodger is such a great part and it was the first time I had to act *and* sing and I loved it, I loved learning the script and trying all the accents, the whole she-bang. Kian was in that too. There was no happier place to be ... not school, football, rugby. None of it came within a whisker of being on stage.

I started to build my confidence and the girls seemed to like my performances, but I knew I must be getting quite good when a few of the lads came up to me and said, 'Shane, that was dead good, fella.'

There was a TV show in Ireland, *says Mark*, called *Go for It*, and they had a sort of 'Name That Tune' segment. At the end, a random member of the public got up and sang a song, sometimes with celebrities. It was brilliant.

I was walking along the street one day with Shane, talking about the show, and I said, 'If they asked us, if our numbers came up, would you go for it with me?'

'Absolutely, I would,' he replied.

At that precise moment, I realized that here was a kid in my neighbourhood who loved singing as much as me and would, given half a chance, literally go for it, and *with me*. I remember walking beside him thinking, *He's cool, everyone likes him, he's an amazing singer and he wants to do something with the singing with me ...*

We'd done *Grease* at the college, *recalls Shane,* and then Mary wanted to put on a bigger version in the town. This was a mixed production, so she was able to bring in girls to sing alongside myself and Kian. She gave Kian and me the role of the T-Birds.

We did our thing and it went down a storm. Everyone was talking about the T-Birds – people proper loved it! So Mary decided to put *Grease* back on in the New Year.

I was doing all these shows, *recalls Kian,* like *Grease, Annie Get Your Gun* and *Oliver,* as well as still playing in rock bands and doing the poetry competitions. It wasn't sneered at for boys to sing in our area, or in Ireland generally. The mixture of Irish musical culture and Sligo's own musical scene meant there were singers everywhere. It was OK for boys to sing.

And in a small-town kinda way, we became sort of famous as the T-Birds. All the girls in the school fancied us. That didn't win us any popularity competitions with the boys, obviously, but we loved it.

All the girls from town did fancy those two, Kian's right, *agrees Mark.* A lot of them were coming to the show just to see Shane and Kian as the T-Birds, that's how good they were.

I wasn't in the T-Birds, but I was still hanging out with everyone in the production. We'd all started getting a bit of a bug for it, it was brilliant. I was seeing quite a bit of Shane by this time and we'd become good friends. One day we were round someone's house watching Boyzone and Take That on the telly, some concert footage, and that's when the idea of starting a boy band came up.

It was very much a group thing; I don't know if any of us would have done it by ourselves. But we were constantly talking about music, singing songs and messing about with pop songs during and after the rehearsals for the various musicals. I realized that although our voices were very different, Shane and me were harmonizing really well. It sounded great. Well, it wasn't that it sounded *amazing*, just that it didn't sound *too* bad! So we started mucking about with the idea of a boy band.

One day, after we'd done the T-Birds thing, *says Kian*, Shane came up to me.

'Hey, Kian, we're thinking of putting a boy band together for the next talent contest and we'd like you to be in it.'

'Are you off your fucking rocker? A boy band? Me? I'm in three rock bands for that talent contest. I'm the lead guitar player in one band, I'm the singer in another band and I'm the guitar player *and* singer in the other band. I can't be in a boy band!'

That was my gut reaction.

Then I heard some tunes by the Backstreet Boys.

Now, you might think it's a big leap from listening to Metallica and Pearl Jam to the Backstreet Boys, and I'll grant you it is. However, the guy behind some of the biggest Backstreet Boys tunes, Max Martin, was a complete metal freak. He loved his rock music and if you listen to those tunes again, you'll hear all sorts of heavy riffing and distortion behind the pop tunes. Maybe nobody else would agree with me on that, but that's why I liked what I heard. It got me intrigued. Suddenly, I quite liked the idea of a boy band. I certainly liked the idea of being in a band that was more popular than Pyromania and in the T-Birds I was getting a reaction on stage like I'd never gotten before just singing and dancing.

So I spoke to Mark and Shane about their band.

That was the start of our first boy band, Six As One.

In the New Year, *says Mark*, the follow-on production of *Grease* was sold out. Because of the reaction to the T-Birds, it had been arranged that during the interval of the show we would come on as this new boy band. There were six of us: myself, Shane, Kian, Derek Lacey, Graham Keighron and Michael 'Miggles' Garrett, all local lads. The plan was to do two songs by the Backstreet Boys, 'I'll Never Break Your Heart' and 'We've Got It Goin' On'.

We weren't sure how people would react, but the place went nuts! Really, it was just the most amazing reaction. We couldn't believe it.

Then Mary suggested that we put on a full concert as Six as One. We rehearsed all day every day for weeks, learning songs by other boy bands. We were really focused.

Come the day of our own show, there were about 500 people in the hall. It felt like about 500,000 – oh my God, it was incredible. The noise they made and the reaction was brilliant. It felt like we were playing Hyde bloody Park! There is actual footage of the gig somewhere and looking at it now it looks really amateur, but it felt so big to us at the time and it was an important starting-point.

It all kind of happened scarily easy. We loved doing it, having some drinks at the weekend and chatting about it too, and there was real ambition there – as soon as that night was over, it was just like, *Right, what are we doing next?*

Mary McDonagh came to us after that concert and suggested we do some recordings. By this point, we'd changed our name to IOYOU. I'd started to write a song called 'Together Girl Forever', which was about Shane's future wife Gillian, but I said to him, 'You're the one who likes her, you write the second verse!'

I was really keen on Gillian by that point, *says Shane*, so it was great to write a song about her. Some of the lads did the music for it and Mark did the lyrics. It wasn't the greatest song you've ever heard – it was all very simple – but it was another step forward. So we took that song and 'Everlasting Love' and another original which featured Graham rapping at one point, and went in to record them.

We were so excited, that was our very first experience of any kind of studio work. It was just a small home studio and the set-up was nothing like the studios we use now, but it was cool. We were singing into mics and listening back and all saying the same thing: 'Do I really sound like that?'

The songs weren't written or produced to the level we are used to now, *says Mark*, but at the time it was all very relevant and important to get us to the next stage. That little phase literally did do wonders for us. Having our own record felt like the biggest deal *ever*. We all had haircuts done especially for the cover. Mine was hideous, so as soon as I could I went to the local barber and had it cut off!

About 100 people bought the record from the store in the first few days, then a few more days went by and another 100 copies sold, then 500, then eventually, after several weeks, we'd shifted about 1,000 of them.

Suddenly, the word of mouth in town was like, 'There's a new boy band and they're from Sligo!' It was all very small scale, but people really got into it, they loved the idea. Mainly girls, actually. At the time, the Backstreet Boys and Boyzone were at their peak, so the idea of Sligo having its own boy band – well, all the local girls loved it.

A while later, Mary McDonagh and her associates offered us a management contract which we had to decide whether to sign or not.

It was an amazing time. It was all a great laugh and yet serious at the same time, we meant business. It seemed so quick too – singing in the interval of *Grease*, then getting our own show, then recording in a studio, then having a record out ... Every step, we felt, *If it all stops tomorrow, this has already been amazing!*

Next thing we knew, we got asked to go on a TV show called *Nationwide*, a magazine show where one week there'd be a young kid doing stunts on a BMX and the next week there'd be an Irish dancing troupe. That week it was us, singing carols in a local children's ward. The TV crew came down and filmed us. They liked it and broadcast the clip at teatime and *everyone* in Sligo seemed to watch it. It was mad. People in the street even started to say hello. 'Hey, that's yer man from that band!'

Oddly, despite going on *Nationwide* and being known as a new local boy band, there was then a bit of an anti-climax, we sort of stalled for a wee while. Shane went to college five hours away from Sligo and we were kinda kicking our heels, like, *That was fun. What now?*

Nicky   Kian   Shane   MARK xx

CHAPTER THREE

A Game of Two Halves

We never wanted for anything in our house, but money certainly didn't grow on trees, *says Dubliner Nicky Byrne.* I think my mam and dad, Nikki and Yvonne Byrne, were very proud parents. My dad was a painter and decorator working in an hotel at Dublin airport and my mam was a housewife. I came into the world on 9 October 1978, my sister Gillian is two years older than me and when I was 11 they had a surprise little brother for us all, Adam. No one knew if we were rich or poor, but if I needed new football boots or Gillian was after some new Irish dancing shoes, we got them.

Growing up, my dad was a singer in a cabaret band. Even to this day he sings. Back then he gigged seven nights of the week, working in lots of pubs and clubs around the city. I loved watching him singing. Sometimes I'd see him go out after dinner to his next show. He'd be wearing his white or blue suits ready for the cabaret. He was the lead singer of Nikki & the Studz and for over ten years they had a residence round the corner in the local pub, the Racecourse in Baldoyle, every Friday, Saturday and Sunday. He used to do a lot of weddings, dinner dances, all that type of thing. He was well known on the Dublin cabaret circuit, me dad. He wasn't a nationally famous singer, but people around and about knew of him. He worked his ass off to provide for us, definitely. He'd take me to football three nights a week and my mam would take Gill to Irish dancing competitions, while having to feed and school us too. It was a busy household.

My dad worked in the Dublin Airport hotel for 17 years before becoming unemployed. I was only a kid and probably didn't understand what being unemployed meant. I heard about it on the news and I know now that there were some horrendous times for people in the 1980s. But as a child, I never felt it, I never saw it, other than on the telly. I remember times when my dad wouldn't be working for a while, then suddenly he'd go out and work on a contract with somebody for, say, six months, then he'd be off work again.

My mam had four sisters – Betty, Marie, Con and Bernadette – and they all had children, our cousins. Every Sunday we'd eat at my nana and granddad's and every Saturday we'd go to my Nana Byrne for her special soup. I have very early memories of crowding around the Christmas tree in Nana and Granddad's tiny living room, opening presents. 'Here you go, Nico. Happy Christmas.' We used to take it in turns each year to hand out the wrapped-up parcels. It's a lovely memory. Everyone got a pressie – even the uncles got socks or 'smellies', as they would say.

My first love was always football. I was a goalkeeper. My dad used to take me to as many games as he could manage. Then he got me into a schoolboy club in Ireland called Home Farm that was quite well known. He took me to training two or three evenings a week and to the matches at weekends, while he was decorating in the day and gigging at night.

I really laugh now, thinking of the car journeys home after we'd lost or I'd made a mistake. While the lads we were dropping off – usually Brian Rickard and Paul Irwin, still mates to this day – were still in the car, Dad would sit there for a while not saying much, then suddenly he'd go, 'What happened there for the second goal, Nico?' There would be a long pause as I thought of an excuse and then he would continue, 'I think you could have probably done better there, son.' It was funny.

Football was my life – I could name the Manchester United team backwards *and* upside down in those days. It meant *everything*. My bedroom wall was covered in posters of football stars – players like Lee Sharpe and Packie Bonner – and there was also one of Kylie Minogue and one of a girl out of *Baywatch* with especially big breasts called Erika Eleniak. It was mainly footballers, though.

I was obviously aware of the big pop bands. My sister wanted to sing; she was a huge Bros fan. She wore the bottle tops on the Dr Martens, the leather jackets, ripped jeans, all of that. Bros were really the guinea pigs for what Take That, Boyzone and Westlife all went on to do. That was when the whole boy band thing first entered my world, I suppose. One Christmas my sister got a three-in-one music player from Santa, which was a cassette player, record player and radio. At first she played Band Aid's 'Do They Know It's Christmas?' then 'When Will I Be Famous?', 'Cat among the Pigeons', all those Bros tunes. As we grew up I would hear A-Ha and Michael Jackson too.

At school, however, music wasn't really my thing. I didn't play an instrument and at that age I wasn't at all interested in the classical music they focused on. My music teacher, Miss Murphy, was lovely and I had a great relationship with her, not because I was particularly musical but more because I was friendly and charming to her, I suppose. I love classical music now – the sound of strings is one of the most beautiful, relaxing things you can hear – but as a kid, you're not interested really, are you?

I was a confident kid, playing football, messing around, having a good time, but I wasn't confident enough to sing in public. I was always in choirs, but that wasn't just me standing there. When it came to my music exam, I was convinced I was going to fail, but luckily 40 per cent of it was practical, just singing. I stood up and sang 'The Fields of Athenry', 'Hey, Jude' and 'Yesterday' by the Beatles and an old Irish song called 'She Moved Through the Fair'. I got full marks and that was enough for me to go on and pass the whole exam. But if I'm being totally honest here, I didn't really have any interest in music whatsoever at that point. It bored me and was a great time to grab a nap in class.

For a while yet, my path was elsewhere, namely football. I was training constantly and getting pretty good. I was playing in better and better teams and people were starting to talk about me as a genuine prospect. My clubs in Dublin were doing well and I progressed enough to get picked for the Ireland Under-15 side, which was a big deal. One of the proudest moments of my life, even to this day, was standing for the Irish national anthem when we played the tournament hosts Portugal in an Under-18 European Championships. There were no Irish fans there and probably about 15,000 Portuguese. All I could think about was my mam and dad, how proud they'd be and how much they'd love to see this. I actually got emotional for the national anthem as we turned to face the Tricolor just like the senior team would do during the World Cup. That moment will never leave me. It was a special time in my football career.

Once you are playing at that level, professional scouts start flying over to watch you and it wasn't long before I was offered a two-week trial at Leeds United. My mam was keen for me to finish my studies, but Dad was like, 'Yes, but it's *Leeds United!*' He felt the same as me. Leeds was one of the top clubs in the UK at the time. Even though I'm a hardcore Man. United fan, this was what I'd dreamed about all my life.

They really liked me at the trial and I was shocked and very, very excited to then be offered a two-year contract for Leeds United FC. I thought this was it, I was made! Any Irish kid who's a big soccer fan wants to get to England to play; the Irish leagues aren't as high profile or as well paid (although, playing in those leagues later, I found them to be amazingly tough and physical, an almost bruising experience).

I'd already started dating a girl from school called Georgina, whose father was Bertie Ahern, the future Prime Minister of Ireland (he was Minister of Finance at the time), so it meant we'd have to conduct a long-distance relationship, which neither of us were very pleased about. We'd been to the same secondary school, Pobailscoil Neasain, and I'd admired her from afar for some time. I remember seeing her on the evening news on the steps of Dail Eireann on budget day with her dad and sister and telling my mam, 'That's the girl I'm going to marry.' I was 12 years old and Mam thought I was nuts. I'd even got my mate to speak to her about going out with me, but the answer came back, 'No.' It was like a dagger through the heart, it really was, I was gutted because I was really falling for this girl. That was about two years after I first saw her. I think we waited another year or two before we arranged to meet at a friend's party on 8 October 1994, the night before my sixteenth birthday – how many guys remember the first date?! – and we kissed and that was it, the love of my life.

Initially, because I was only 16, I was on a YTS scheme at Leeds, getting £38.50 a week, but as soon as I turned 17 and signed as a professional, I was paid £200 a week for year one then £250 for year two and had free digs, so suddenly I felt rich. Having a bit of spare cash, I was starting to wear a few labels like Dolce & Gabbana, plus I'd got a £5,000 signing-on fee, so it felt amazing.

But then the reality hit home. At first, we stayed in Roundhay in Leeds with a lovely couple called Pete and Maureen Gunby. He was a former Leeds coach. They were really nice to all the players staying with them. In year two, we were moved to lodgings in a purpose-built complex at the new training ground in Thorpe Arch near Weatherby. The digs were like army barracks. There was a strict curfew on nights out and anyone breaking that was disciplined. It was the closest thing to a prison. In the second year, they installed cameras in the corridors outside our rooms. As soon as the door slammed shut, the dream evaporated and you were in these pretty spartan digs, two lads per room. I had a family picture on my dresser and the Tricolor above my bed and a picture of Roy Keane on me wall, but that was as homely as it got. You went up for your food on a tray and sat down to eat in the canteen.

They dished out proper bollockings if you did something wrong – shouting matches, the works. It was a real shock to the system and I got homesick very badly. That second year nearly broke me. I don't think I ever thought about actually walking – I never had the balls to go home and throw the towel in, that never crossed my

WESTLIFE – OUR STORY | 41

mind, I probably should have but I was determined that it wasn't going to break me – but it did get me pretty down.

One night us Irish lads went out and got pissed. The next morning we were frog-marched into the office and our contracts laid out on the table in front of us. They were sacking us. The coach in charge was shouting in our faces, but it turned out to be a scare tactic. As I wiped the spit from my face and looked around at the other lads, I realized it was working.

It had started so well. Although I was only a junior, just a few months out of school, through a series of injuries to goalkeepers, more senior than me, I was named in the first team squad for a match at Southampton. It was incredible – I was on the first-team coach with all the professionals, big-name players I'd seen on the telly like Gary McAllister, Tony Yeboah, Gary Speed and the Irish legend Gary Kelly and now I was in the squad with them. I didn't play that day, but it was such a buzz to be even near that level of football. Mam and Dad kept all the paper clippings from back home and even recorded the news on Teletext, they were so proud.

But the honeymoon period didn't last for long. The problem I had was that I flitted in and out of the team. When that happens, especially as a goalkeeper, football is a very lonely place. When you're not in the team at that level, often not even as a substitute, you're nothing more than a boot boy, a drinks boy, pushing skips around with kit in them, like. Sometimes players' faces fit and sometimes they don't. It's the same in any job, the same in boy bands ...

One of the few highlights of my time at Leeds was the magic phone. One day, my room-mate Keith Espey went to ring his mum, but the payphone didn't seem to be working and he was pressing the number 7 in frustration – you know, 'Come on! Work!' Then the phone rang, he picked it up and it was his mum. 'Did you just try to call me?' she said.

Turned out her phone had rung after all, but for some reason Keith hadn't had to put any money in. His mum checked on her next bill and there was no sign of the call being reverse charged or anything like that. So we all started doing it – pick up the phone, bang it back down, 7777, wait a few seconds, phone rings, make your call. I was phoning Ireland and we had Welsh lads phoning Wales. Even Harry Kewell,the future Liverpool player who was from Australia, was calling home. It was brilliant!

This was one of the rare highlights, though, as I said. Mentally, those years at Leeds were the toughest time in my whole life. I didn't get on with the coach, I was only allowed six paid visits home a year, I was homesick and I wasn't getting picked. The rules were ludicrous – for example if I didn't shave, I was fined a fiver. There were times when I thought to myself, *What am I serving my sentence for?* When you are away you get very patriotic and I got very homesick and used to play a lot of Boyzone, funnily enough – 'Father and Son', tunes like that. Even more bizarrely, I saw Mikey from that band in a club one night in Howth, County Dublin, surrounded by girls, and that image stuck with me.

By the Christmas of 1997 I knew I was finished with football. My height – 5ft 10in – worked against me, as most modern professional goalkeepers are well over six foot. But also my face and personality weren't fitting in with certain people at Leeds United, as I said, and I could see the end was coming. Still, I was devastated. This had been my dream since I was knee-high and it was falling apart.

Even the way they broke the news was typical – they said I was one of the best prospects they'd ever seen, but I needed to grow a few inches and that if I didn't between then and the end of my contract, it wouldn't be renewed. I was 19. It wasn't going to happen. Then, when the time came to leave, there wasn't even a handshake.

My confidence was ruined as a footballer. I'm a very confident person – my mam and dad gave us a really good upbringing and filled us all with confidence – but after Leeds, that had gone, with regards to football at least. There were options: playing in the part-time Irish leagues (I eventually did play for Shelbourne, Cobh Ramblers and St Francis) or playing for English clubs further down the tables like Cambridge or Scarborough. I did try out for a couple, but I wasn't interested. My heart wasn't in it anymore.

I retreated to Dublin, gutted. My football dream was over.

To be honest with you, I was dying to get home.

CHAPTER FOUR

LARGER THAN LIFE

The phone rings.

'Hello, Shane, it's Mam. How are you?'

'Fine, Mam, thanks. Are you OK?'

'Good, thanks. Listen, I've been on the phone with Boyzone's manager, that Louis Walsh, and ...'

'What?! Mam, go away, will ya?'

I thought she was joking. I hung up on her.

The phone rings again.

'Shane, listen, I've been on the phone with that Louis Walsh. I've been phoning for months trying to get hold of him and I just finally spoke to him about your band.'

She wasn't joking.

It turned out that she had indeed spoken with Louis Walsh, manager of Boyzone and one of the most powerful men in the music business. Mam came from the same small village as him, Kiltimagh in County Mayo, and to her, there was no reason why she shouldn't

phone this famous manager and tell him about her son's band. They
didn't know each other personally, they'd never met even, but her
family knew of his family, it was that kind of village, literally in the
middle of nowhere. So she'd just gone straight to the top of the food
chain.

She'd rung for months and he hadn't answered – not surprising
really, given that Boyzone were absolutely massive at the time. But
eventually, one day, Louis just picked the phone up.

'Hello?'

Mam had introduced herself then had charmed her way
through. 'I can't believe you're on the phone, I've been trying for
months ...'

'Sorry, I'm away on business a lot. What can I do for you?'

'It's my son,' explained Mam. 'He's in this boy band called
IOYOU.'

'I know, I've heard of them,' said Louis.

When my mum told me all this, you could have knocked me
down with a feather. He'd seen us on *Nationwide*.

Mam explained all this to me then said, 'You've got a meeting
with him tomorrow night.'

Jesus.

'A meeting with Louis Walsh?'

'Yes.'

'As in Boyzone's fuc ...' I nearly swore, '... manager.'

'Yes, Shane.'

'Are you after having me on?'

She wasn't.

Me and Kian went and met Louis Walsh, as in 'Boyzone's-fucking-manager'. I'd never even seen him before because, although he was well known in Ireland, he hadn't yet been on *X Factor* or the telly in general. I expected some great big manager with a ponytail, the sort of guy that, as a teenager, I'd imagined looked after Michael Jackson.

My mum had just asked if Louis would meet up with us and give us some advice, which he very kindly did. He said he wasn't looking to manage a new band because Boyzone were exploding all over the place and he was too busy with that. I gave him our CD, he looked at the cover and said that six lads in a boy band was too many.

We explained that we'd been offered a management contract by Mary and he asked if we'd taken legal advice and who from. It was great stuff – really good of him to lend us his ear and give us some direction. Then he gave us his phone number – Louis Walsh as in 'Boyzone's-fucking-manager's' phone number – and said to call if we needed any more advice.

A few days later, my phone rang. It was Louis.

'Hey, Shane, I've got an invite for you and one of the lads to Ronan Keating's 21st birthday party ...'

At the time, aside from Bono, there was no bigger name in Irish music than Ronan Keating. So along with Michael, I went to Ronan's party. This was only two weeks after my mum had finally spoken to Louis on the phone. We met Ronan – he came in on a big Harley Davidson motorbike with his soon-to-be wife Yvonne on the back. Louis was there, too, obviously, so we also spoke to him again.

After a while, I needed the toilet so I went to the gents and was amazed to see Ken Doherty, the snooker world champion, standing at the loo. I nervously stood next to him and was going about my business when I heard a voice say, 'Hey, Ken, how you doing, man?' I looked across and Alan Shearer was standing there taking a piss.

We had a band meeting not long after, all six of us sitting around in my parents' café, which was our meeting spot. We were discussing what Louis Walsh might or might not do to help us. The main topic of conversation was that he didn't see a future for a boy band with six members. We all talked about it and agreed we couldn't turn down the chance of Louis Walsh being involved in some way, even if it was just to find us a good manager somewhere else. We just sensed Louis might be involved somehow and that it was too big an opportunity to miss. So we agreed, there and then, to just go for it. If one of us had to go, then so be it. We kind of all knew somebody would get cut – Boyzone, Backstreet Boys, N*Sync, Take That, Five, there were plenty of examples – and we were all happy with that decision.

Looking back, I think Louis genuinely didn't want to be involved in a boy band with six members, but I also think he was fishing to see how much we wanted it and whether we would be good to work with. Remember, he hadn't even seen us perform live at this stage.

By now we kinda knew that the contract we'd been offered by Mary McDonagh wasn't going to happen. At the same time, being in contact with Louis Walsh made us feel that we might only have one shot at it and we wanted it to be brilliant. So we ended up not signing the first contract and obviously fell out with those people over it. We didn't want to fall out with them, but they obviously weren't happy about it and, looking back, I totally understand that.

When we had meetings about Mary's contract, *says Mark*, I sort of sat in the corner and hoped that the majority would make the decision for me and that it would be the right choice. I didn't want to get into a fight because I've always hated confrontation. But when we said we didn't want to sign, that relationship was pretty much over.

It's a very difficult subject because I have an awful lot of love, respect and admiration for Mary. I always looked up to her and wanted her approval, but there was the situation with Louis Walsh developing and also we were not all happy with the contract.

That was a tricky time, because at such a young age it was the first real time we'd had to confront a situation like that, the first big, major, adult decision outside school or family life.

I sometimes think about and still feel bad for Mary and the other people, *says Shane*, because she was a good friend. I see her around town from time to time now and I go to productions of my cousin's back home. Sadly, I haven't talked to her in ten years, though, not a word. I have great respect for her and view her as a person who did a lot for me when I was younger – when it came to my performance, she helped me a lot.

What I will say is that, as Mark mentioned, this was the first time that the music business lunged into our cosy little Sligo life. Making the decision not to go with Mary and then working with Louis later, it was like, *Jesus, this shit is cut-throat.*

When we said we were sorry but we couldn't sign the contract with her, they were very sore about it for a long time, but it was just a decision we had to make. I had to make it for my life and my family and any future family. We weren't saying no to Mary to go instead with any old manager, it was *Louis Walsh*. I'd like to think they would have done the exact same thing if the tables were turned the other way around. He was probably the best pop manager in Europe at the time. We just couldn't turn down that chance.

By the time Louis Walsh got involved, *says Kian*, I was ready to walk out of education, I was ready to give it up. I was 'Let's go, go, go!'

For Mark and Shane, it was a little trickier. They wanted it every bit as much as me, but they were good at school and they had their exams to consider. I was like, 'Forget about exams!' I never had any interest in class, I wasn't into the studying and learning languages, all that. I went to school for the activities afterwards – the sports, the drama, the acting and the singing. All I wanted in life was to be on a stage, singing in a big band.

The phone rings.

'Is that your phone, Shane?'

We were all sitting in the pub, having a pint and a laugh.

We'd all only just got mobiles, so no one knew whose ringtone it was, and we were scraping around trying to find the right phone.

It was mine.

Hardly anyone knew our numbers yet and I could see it was a Dublin number and I thought, *Who the fuck is this?*

'Hello?'

'Hello, Shane, it's Louis Walsh. Listen, are you guys doing anything on Saturday night?'

'Er, no, I don't think so, Louis. Why? What's happening?'

All the lads gathered around me when they heard me say his name.

'Well, how would you like to support the Backstreet Boys in three days' time?'

'What?!'

'For two nights.'

CHAPTER FIVE

RECKONING

'Are you serious, Louis?' I had grabbed Shane's phone, *recalls Kian.*

'Deadly serious!' He was chuckling, he could hear my excitement.

'Don't be messing with us ...'

'Kian, I am not messing, get yourself on a train!'

I can't tell you how exciting that was. I used to say, 'I don't want to be in a Boyzone, I want to be in the next Backstreet Boys,' because they were the ones I really looked up to. Them and Take That, mainly. Same for the other two lads.

Before I even try to explain the state of absolute shock, joy and bewilderment that came over us all, let me backtrack six months to a street in town, with a ticket booth about to put tickets to see the Backstreet Boys on sale. Me and Shane had queued from the middle of the night to get those tickets. The booth didn't open until 9 a.m., but we were there from 4 a.m. just to make sure.

When Louis called about the support slot, *remembers Mark*, I'd just been in McDonald's with a girl called Avril and Gillian, talking about how exciting it was that we were going to see the Backstreet Boys concert at the weekend.

When we got those bits of paper saying 'Backstreet Boys + Support', *recalls Shane*, it was like finding Willy Wonka's golden ticket, we were so pleased. So fast-forward to the pub around that table when Louis had told us he'd got a slot for our band supporting the Backstreet Boys. I'll never forget it – it was one of the best moments of my life. Gillian was upstairs waitressing and we all ran up there screaming the news, jumping up and down, crying, laughing, shouting! It was crazy.

After we'd calmed down, I remember thinking, *How is this going to work? I'm going to meet the Backstreet Boys. I'm going to shake their hands, maybe even talk to them.* It was just so surreal. *And we don't need those tickets that we queued for anymore …*

I'd just left college, where I'd been doing a business and accounting course which I hated (maths and accountancy were the only two things I did very well at in school – I got As in both). It was in Limerick and I badly missed home, I didn't like the course and I just wanted out. So I came home and got a job at a builder's provider called Buckley's, just lifting boxes around, odd jobs. My father knew the man who owned it, Stanley, and one of my best friends, Paul Keaveney, worked there too. I used to go out the back singing these Backstreet Boys songs and they used to rip the piss out of me. Now we were going to be supporting them.

I felt like we'd won the lottery. I knew we were a long way from being a success yet – we weren't that naïve – but if nothing else it was confirmation that Louis Walsh was going to be involved, and as far as we were concerned that *was* the winning lottery ticket. We'd struck gold – not just the support slot, but having Louis on our side. Even that early on, we just sensed that something was happening. There were too many things going our way. We felt that our winning numbers had come up.

At the time I was working in our local jeans shop, *says Kian*, called EJ's Menswear. You can imagine the reaction of the owner, Eamonn Cunningham, when I said, 'I could do with some decent clothes this weekend. We're supporting the Backstreet Boys!' He was very helpful and let us all go round on an evening and try out all this Sonnetti and Firetrap gear, big orange jackets and white jeans. It was so exciting.

So, anyway, we had three days to the Backstreet Boys' support slot. Three days!

Luckily, we already had several routines well rehearsed, so it wasn't as bad as we first thought.

On the day of the show we met the Backstreet Boys and there was absolutely no hint of us acting cool – we were just proper fans all excited to meet them. We got them to sign albums for us and said thanks for offering the slot – they could have said no, they could have asked for a band with a record deal, for example. Plenty of stars do.

The Backstreet Boys loaded up on the Friday night and we were already outside, too excited to stay away. I vividly recall standing at the windows, peering through. There we were, all our faces squashed against the glass, and the Backstreet Boys were inside playing basketball. We couldn't believe we could actually see them with our own eyes, that's how famous they were to us.

At that window, looking in, *remembers Mark*, I was phoning my friends, saying, 'I can see AJ, he's got two eight-foot tall security guards walking with him. He looks really small ... Oh, now I can see Brian!'

We were such wide-eyed fans. But within a few hours we were chatting to the band and eating with them. It was so weird – but brilliant weird!

The night of the gig came around, *says Shane*, our little slot came up and we walked on. There were about 6,000 people in the audience. The most we'd ever played in front of before was a few hundred. We did 'Together Girl Forever', 'Everlasting Love', complete with Graham's little rap, and 'Pinball Wizard' by the Who. It was mental, a real laugh. The crowd were roaring and screaming. They went mental for us because we were an Irish band. They just loved it. I'll never forget it.

For those shows, we were staying at the Mount Herbert Hotel. It was like a massive B&B. There was the six of us packed into one room. We had no money; our parents were even paying for the room. We literally didn't have a bean between us.

That first night was Paddy's night, so we had a few beers. It just seemed too good to be true.

Then one of the Backstreet Boys said, 'Hey, Mark, we're going to the pub tomorrow after the show. You should come,' and we were like, 'Are you for real?'

So next thing I know, we're at this club chatting with Howie and Kevin over a pint. It was all a bit of a blur, to be honest with you.

Kian remembers that it was about to get even better: That night at the gig, Louis took me to one side and said, 'I want to manage you.'

What we hadn't known was that Louis had been pretty much auditioning us at the show, to see whether he wanted to become our manager or not. He did and we couldn't believe our ears.

However, there was a catch.

'I think you have something special, Kian, but I want you to lose the big guy.'

I said, 'You can't cut Mark!' At this point Mark was a big lad – not overweight, he was just a big lad.

'No, Mark's amazing. I'm talking about Derek.'

Derek was six foot tall and muscular, in really good shape. I thought he had a good dark look, personally. But Louis still didn't want six members in the band and, worse still, he said that he didn't think Derek was suitable. There was no compromise, it had to be just five.

Even though we'd all agreed to go forward knowing someone might get cut, it was still devastating when it came to it. Derek was probably Shane's best friend in the band at the time, so he was gutted.

It was a big shock, *agrees Mark*. Even though the group was slowly morphing itself into a professional, 'real' band, it was still literally made up of childhood schoolmates. So it was a very strange and difficult situation.

Louis has always been brutally honest. I've long since got used to that, but at first the way he spoke about the situation with Derek seemed so harsh to me. I was used to the country life near Sligo and there everyone was very friendly. If you went into the grocer's and he was grumpy, rather than think, *Wanker*, you'd think, *He must have had a bad night's sleep.* It was all very pure. It wasn't like *Alice in Wonderland,* but everyone was really genuine. So then Louis Walsh turned up and started saying things like, 'You're a bit fat, and you should get your hair cut,' it took me back. I wasn't equipped to deal with that approach. I was never taught how to deal with people speaking to me like that.

I've got to point out here that this isn't just Louis, it's basically how the record industry operates. It is very direct. I'm jumping ahead of the story a little here, but I remember there was a girl who worked on reception at a record company office and she was morbidly obese. I'd go in and she'd be on the phone saying, 'Right, Mark's going to the gym now ...' and I'd feel like saying, 'Are *you* going to the fucking gym?' That's the nature of the industry and I understand that now – the point was that she wasn't on TV and she wasn't the face in a boy band, but at the time I took everything personally.

When Louis said he didn't think Derek was suitable, it was a major problem.

I was the one who told Derek, *says Shane.* I felt that I should be the one because he was such a good friend. All the band were there, sitting around, and I said, 'Louis wants five in the band and he just thinks you're not suited to the group.'

It is probably the hardest thing I have ever had to do in my life. It was awful.

Derek was visibly upset, understandably, and walked out the room.

I'm sad to say that we didn't speak for the longest time after that – not for years. He obviously felt he couldn't be my friend anymore. It got worse when Westlife went on to be a big success – that must have been tough for Derek to see. I personally would have hated the band, I would have hated Westlife. He probably did for a long time and I don't blame him.

I hope he doesn't now. I do chat to him occasionally and see him now and then. I've even been out with him a couple of times. But for a long time nobody talked. It was a tough call. Derek is a great guy.

I didn't say much at all when Shane told him, *recounts Mark*. I think I went and put my hand on his shoulder at the door. But I've spoke to him since and I've cleared things up as much as I can. It's always going to be pretty awkward.

*   *   *

Shane: About two months later, I thought I was next for the chop. Louis had arranged an audition for a man from Sony-BMG. We travelled up to Dublin and had a few beers the night before to settle the nerves. Well, actually, that's not strictly true. We'd all agreed to go easy in the pubs, but it was a night out in Sligo and you don't want to miss the Friday night, you know. We met up with some people and there was a big party and, anyway, look, the long and short of it is, I was a bit steamed. The night before an audition, with an 8.30 morning train, what was I thinking?

We got on the train and met Louis at the audition. We went into this room at the Westbury hotel and then this man came in with black hair wearing really high-waisted black trousers. I didn't know him at all.

'Hello, I'm Simon Cowell. Pleased to meet you.'

Mark: I was like, *God, he's a bit posh, a bit cocky.* I didn't even know what 'A&R' meant. I just thought he owned Sony-BMG.

I was nervous at that audition, *remembers Shane*, but not because of Simon. He wasn't famous at all at this stage, he was just a successful A&R man from Sony. His big band of the time was Five, so we knew he would be great to work with. The room was tiny; we were standing pretty much next to him and Louis.

I performed terribly.

The rest of the lads were great, but I knew I hadn't done the job.

Simon seemed unimpressed, spoke briefly with Louis and then Louis gestured us into another room.

As I came out of the audition room, Louis grabbed me and kinda half-hit me – not a slap or punch, just in exasperation.

'What the fuck was that, Shane? It was shite. He doesn't like ya.'

Louis was really mad at me. I'd never seen him like that before and I was so shocked. He was so passionate about the band and he was so into what he was doing, he couldn't believe I'd been so poor for Simon Cowell.

'I was counting on you and you let me down. You look terrible, what's up with ya?'

'Well, I had a few last night and ...'

'*What?!*'

He was just raging at me and I was apologizing, because I knew he was right.

He told us that Simon actually only liked Kian and Mark and particularly didn't like me. I later found out that when Simon had said he didn't like me, Louis had said, 'Well, I think he's a star,' to which Simon had replied, 'Well, he wasn't a star here today, Louis.'

Louis had then spoken with Simon in private and told him he'd get new members in, he'd work on the band and sort it all out and if Simon would come back one more time, he'd love it.

'OK, but only because it's you, Louis,' said Simon, and then he left.

My whole future flashed before me. I thought, *It's over, it's over. Louis is going to tell me to get back on the train and piss off.*

'I know you can be a star,' Louis said to me. 'I believe in you too much, so sort your life out and don't come up here looking shite again.'

His reaction sounds harsh, but d'you know what? It gave me the biggest kick in the arse that I'd ever got. I thought I'd blown everything and then for Louis to say what he did, I felt like I was being given a lifeline.

Louis wasn't about to let the momentum stall, *explains Kian,* so he sent us to London to record some songs with an up-and-coming songwriter called Steve Mac. He told us this guy could write brilliant pop songs and we were all very excited.

When we got there, we all sang. He listened to each of us carefully and then we recorded three songs, 'Everybody Knows', 'The Good Thing' and 'Forever', all Steve Mac/Wayne Hector songs. The idea was that we'd have some good strong material for our next phase of showcasing for labels.

There was such a buzz around Steve Mac, you just knew he was going to go somewhere, *recalls Shane.* We'd done those songs in the small studio back in Sligo, but nothing like this – it looked like a spaceship in there.

We were really nervous going in, obviously. We were new to the game and I wondered, *What's yer man gonna think of us?* After all, the whole industry was talking about him. I thought he'd soon be talking about *us,* saying, *This lot are shite.*

As it turned out, he was very complimentary. It was great. He loved our singing.

That was the first time we'd had such nice things said by a professional in a studio at that level and it did us the world of good. For me personally, that was a massive boost.

Then, BANG, another shock, *explains Kian*. A short while after the disastrous audition for Simon Cowell, Louis said to me, 'Listen, Kian, I don't think Graham is right for the band either.'

I was like, 'Jesus, no.'

Louis explained his concerns and I asked if he was certain. He said he knew what the music business wanted and that Graham didn't quite fit into that.

I was devastated. Graham was my old mate, we were really good friends. I was like, 'Oh, Louis, don't be doing this, please.' But at the end of the day, what could I do?

I did try to keep Graham in the band for as long as possible. It was very hard for me, that phase. We even put on a gig at the Sligo Arts Festival, videoed it and sent the tape to Louis to prove that Graham was good enough to be in the band. It was at my local community hall and I thought Graham was great.

I don't know whether Louis watched the video or not, but he hadn't changed his mind the next time I spoke to him.

Graham knew this was all going on, he knew what Louis had been saying, but it was still really hard.

Shane had been really upset telling Derek and he didn't want to do it again, so Louis agreed to make the call, which he did one night when Graham was round my house. Graham went upstairs to my little brother's box bedroom to take the call. Louis was very careful how he said it. He told him, 'Graham, I think you should step back from this. I don't think you're right, I'm afraid, but I want you to be the tour manager.'

That was a nice touch and I was pleased that Graham could still be involved. I didn't actually know what a tour manager was; I was just pleased Graham was still around.

You have to take your hat off to Graham for his reaction to it all. Bear in mind we'd already supported the Backstreet Boys and Louis was one of the biggest pop managers on the planet. Graham knew there was a very good chance it was going to go big. And yet, despite all this, when Louis mentioned the tour manager's role, he was like, 'Great, I'll have a crack at that.' Brilliant reaction. I'd have said, 'Stuff your fucking tour manager's job!' but Graham was bigger than that. Fair play to him.

The problem was, now we were only a four-piece again: Michael, me, Mark and Shane.

Louis was already on it. He wanted to hold auditions for a fifth member.

I know this might sound really callous, but to a degree, we would have done almost anything Louis Walsh asked of us at this point. He was the man, he was the biggest boy band manager in Europe and here he was working with us. We were kids, we felt that something was happening and, don't forget, we'd all agreed that we would carry on, knowing that things might get difficult and there might be casualties. So we'd have done almost anything.

Although I don't think, *says Shane*, I'd have worn shiny hot pants, to be fair with you.

MARK xx

CHAPTER SIX

THE BIGGEST PUB BAND IN THE WORLD

Even though I was still young when I left Leeds United, *recalls Nicky*, I'd become used to a nice lifestyle. Also, I'm a very proud person and I didn't want anyone to think I'd failed. I especially didn't want my mam and dad thinking I'd failed. But I didn't know what I wanted to do next. Ever since I was a kid, apart from football, I'd wanted to be a copper. But I wasn't really sure what was going to happen next.

I did a repeat year at Plunkett College in White Hall and started playing for Shelbourne FC, one of the big clubs in Ireland ('Shelbourne Sign Irish Ace!' read their bulletin headline, then people read it and thought, *Who the fuck is he?*) But I was doing too much – working, studying, training. It was no good.

I'd landed back in Ireland with about ten grand in my bank account. Despite my disappointment at the way things had turned out, at least the money meant I didn't have to rush my next move. I got a job at Alias Tom's clothes shop in Dublin city centre which paid £150 a week and toyed with the idea of buying a Suzuki Vitara Jeep with most of the ten grand, but ended up spending £400 to insure me dad's Seat Cordova. Dad loved it because I was able to drive him to his gigs at night and he could have a drink, and I loved it because once I'd dropped him off, usually about 7 p.m., I had a car for the evening.

While I was passing my exams, I'd started singing in karaoke bars. I'd be working late in Alias Tom's, get home, have my dinner, get changed, miss football training and go to karaoke instead. After a while, I was confident enough to enter some karaoke competitions and I did OK, getting to some semi-finals and the odd final. Funnily enough, I was almost always singing Take That and Boyzone songs. I'd played Boyzone a lot when I was at Leeds United. Songs like 'Father and Son' really made me miss home. The players used to take the piss out of me and call me Ronan, even. Georgina's dad had met the band somewhere and he'd even got her a signed album, which we listened to non-stop. They were the songs I knew, they were the songs I was listening to. I didn't really listen to the Backstreet Boys. It wasn't that I didn't like them, I just didn't know much about them and I liked backing the Irish boys. A lot of fellas were into Boyzone; it wasn't uncool to like them.

One day I rang my dad and said, 'Listen, if I buy a karaoke machine and some discs out of the money I've got left over from Leeds, will you come around with me when you're not gigging your own shows? We'll try and book a few venues that do karaoke.'

He loved the idea, so we started playing shows where I'd present and sing two songs, then he'd do two songs, then we'd start asking the audience to come up and do a song. Suddenly I was working the clubs.

I got all these 'business' cards printed. We were called – genius idea – Father and Son Karaoke.

I was honestly starting to think about going down the road my dad had taken. I was looking to get a band together too and hopefully start working like that.

My normal day would consist of dropping Dad off at work, going to school, finishing there mid-afternoon, then heading up to the suburbs of north Dublin, where I doorstepped pretty much every pub in the area. I'd meet the manager, give them my card, tell them we'd been doing this for years and years, chat about playing for Leeds and just generally use a bit of banter to get work. We got a couple of college socials through friends, then we got our first ever Friday night at the local pub, Gibneys, in Malahide, through a friend of mine and Georgina's at school.

One day Georgina phoned me and said, 'My auntie's just heard something about auditions for a new band.'

It turned out someone was forming a traditional Irish boy band playing old instruments and singing classic Irish folk songs. I got all the info and it just asked for a picture and a demo tape and stated that playing an instrument would be preferable but not essential.

Georgina's sister, the novelist Cecelia Ahern, had been a big Take That fan, so that meant I'd been listening to more and more of this boy band stuff. I remember watching Take That on *Top of the Pops* and that's the first time I started to admit to liking the idea of being in a boy band. I sat there and thought to myself, *Five lads, touring the world, making loads of money, girls everywhere, they must be having a right craic.* I even went to the barbers one day and asked for Jason Orange's haircut.

So now, a few years later, I decided to give it a go. I don't know if it was the fame game or money or success or all of it rolled into one that I craved. I was definitely into the music thing by this point, even though I didn't have a lot of experience.

Funnily enough, I'd recently seen a photo in the *Evening Herald* of this new boy band – six lads called IOYOU. I didn't recognize any of them and didn't think anything more of it. It just said Louis Walsh had given them a slot supporting the Backstreet Boys. It sounded like they would do well. I thought, *Lucky bastards.*

Back in the week before my audition for the traditional band, I didn't have a demo tape, so my dad got our karaoke microphones out and set them up in the front room. Dad, Georgina and my little brother Adam were there. They kept laughing at me and I was getting really irate. I kept pressing 'Stop' halfway through a song and starting again.

Eventually I got a demo finished. It was a pretty rough recording, but it was good enough. It included 'Scorn Not his Simplicity', a pretty sad song about a Down's Syndrome child, and 'Father and Son' by Boyzone. Previously, I'd paid £100 to have some photos taken for a modelling agency who then never called me back, so I used those professional shots for this audition package and sent it all off.

Then one day this guy phoned the house and asked me along to the auditions at the Pod. My mam was going for a test on her throat that day, so I was a bit worried about her, and I hadn't told anyone I was going for the audition. So I just got on the train into town wearing a black shiny suit and a royal blue tie, I really dressed smart. I like dressing up for certain occasions and I figured that with Boyzone, every time you saw them they were wearing shirts and ties.

There were hundreds of lads in the queue for the audition with numbers stuck to them, just like you see on the *X Factor* auditions nowadays. I was number 18, and number 12 was a lad called Brian McFadden. I'd seen this tall, bleached blond guy already – he just stood out a mile. He looked a little like Nick Carter from the Backstreet Boys and he just seemed a little more funky than the rest of the queue. I stood there and thought, *Shite, he already looks like a member of a boy band.* It's weird, because I don't remember anyone else in the whole room.

Brian came over to me – which was equally weird, because I'd never met him before – and said, 'You sing out in the Swords Manor, don't you?' It turned out he'd seen me doing karaoke in the pubs out there. 'A couple of the lads over there are talking about you. They've heard you sing.'

Brian got up and sang before me and he was good. He was very good. He had the look, he was confident and I thought to myself, *Jesus, he's good. I wouldn't mind being in a band with him.* Prior to Brian, guys had been up there playing violins and pianos, slaughtering Corrs songs, so he stood out a mile.

When it came to my turn, I stood up ready to sing 'Father and Son'. There's a four bar intro before the opening line; now, I'd sung this a thousand times in karaoke bars, I knew it inside out, but for some reason, I completely fluffed it by coming in after two bars. I wasn't experienced enough to recover it, so I just blocked out the music and carried on singing. I could see a man standing on the judging panel waving his hand at his throat, gesturing to cut the audition music, but I just kept singing.

And the judges kept listening.

Then they cut the music.

I kept singing, *a capella*.

They kept listening. For most of the song.

I knew it was a good sign, because some of the previous audition-ees hadn't lasted a verse before the dreaded, 'Thank you very much. Next!'

I'd heard one of the men on the panel was Louis Walsh. I knew his name, but I didn't know what he looked like. He'd been asked by the man forming the traditional boy band to help him, given Boy-zone's huge profile at the time. In fact, what Louis had also done was take the opportunity to scout for new talent to complete the line-up for Westlife.

Louis had invited me to these auditions after we'd cut Graham, *explains Kian*. I was sitting there watching all these lads singing, armed with my Filofax, all organized, taking the numbers of the guys we liked. Louis really liked Nicky straight away. He was dressed in a suit, he looked quite smart and he had a really good attitude about him and a great look. You could tell he knew what he wanted and he came across as being a wee bit more mature than some of the others.

Brian seemed as mad as a hatter – but in a good way! He had these big baggy jeans on and a funky jacket and was all blah, blah, blah, talking 500 miles an hour. Both of those lads were brilliant.

I was walking up the stairs to leave, *continues Nicky*, when someone said, 'They want you to stay behind a while, if you don't mind.'

I was taken to another part of the club and there, already waiting, was Brian McFadden. Then a security man came over and explained that Louis Walsh wanted to talk to me. I knew then that I was in with a chance, this had to be a good sign.

I'd never met Louis before and he came right up to me, talking really fast. I tried to catch what he was saying.

'Hello, Nicky, how are you? My name's Louis Walsh and I'm putting together a new pub band and I'd like you to be in it.'

I didn't want to be in a pub band, but this was Louis Walsh, you know, yer man with Boyzone.

'OK, great. Yes.'

Louis was off again, speaking like a machine gun, and all I could do was say, 'Yes,' while all the time thinking, *I don't want to be in a pub band. My mates don't know I'm here, there seems to be a film crew outside and I'm gonna go home and announce I've got a job in a pub band.*

'... so if you'd wait around please, Nicky,' Louis continued, 'we'd like to get some photos of you before you leave.'

The photographer came over and Louis said, as bold as brass, 'This is Nicky Byrne and he's going to be in my new pub band,' and with that, he left. It was like a whirlwind leaving the building.

Then Kian Egan walked over and introduced himself.

I didn't know him from Adam. It was the first time I'd set eyes on him.

'Hi, I'm Kian Egan and I'm in a band called IOYOU. Louis is going to manage us and we are looking for one other person.'

'Is this the pub band Louis has been telling me about?' I asked.

'No, no, away with ya, we're a pop band.'

'Aaahhhh, a *pop* band. Fucking hell, that's a big difference!'

'Louis really likes you,' said Kian, 'and we're going to be holding auditions. There are a few other people here he likes, but he really likes you, you're his favourite. What's your plan for the rest of the day ...?'

Shane: So Louis had scaled it down to about 60 lads and then we had to go and audition them in Dublin. It was exactly like *X Factor* – we all sat there in front of these guys who came in and sang for us.

Brian McFadden was the first person on stage and Nicky Byrne was the second.

Every single lad who came on after that, we all just kept comparing them to Brian and Nicky. There were plenty of good-looking fellas, and great singers too, but none of them made as much impact as Brian and Nicky. Louis felt that myself and Mark had lead vocals, so we wanted two lads who could sing, but also there was a lot of pressure on them to fit in with the look that he wanted. The few that we chose then came and spoke to us and it was still just between Nicky and Brian.

I really got on with Brian while we were auditioning, *continues Nicky,* so we'd swapped phone numbers. Then he rang and we arranged to meet up. The night before singing in front of IOYOU, Brian and me had done karaoke together at a local pub and he was brilliant. He sang the Backstreet Boys song 'Quit Playing Games' and I was after singing Boyzone numbers. I put my money on Boyzone coming up the next day.

So then at the audition all the lads from Sligo – Kian, Shane, Mark and Michael – said to me, 'Right, come upstairs, just us lot. We're going to do some songs with you.'

I was thinking, *Please be Boyzone songs, please be Boyzone songs ...*

'Right,' said Kian, 'we're gonna be singing some Backstreet Boys songs ...'

Shite.

'Do you know "Quit Playing Games"?'

Thank God for that.

I sang melody with them and then Brian went up and he sang too. He was very good.

Brian had blond curtains for hair, *remembers Kian,* so he did indeed look like Nick Carter. This was the way we were thinking: we weren't thinking small scale at all, we were thinking of the big fish. I loved Brian's vibe and look, and he could really sing, but I was unsure about him being so lively. 'I don't know,' I said, 'he's mad!'

Fortunately, the rest of the band persuaded me that he could be brilliant – and they were right. I was all for Nicky – he was great, sang well, looked perfect, he was the one as far as I was concerned. It was those two by a mile we wanted to choose the new member from, but there was a complication: Shane and Mark favoured Brian; Louis and myself favoured Nicky.

They were both good-looking lads and Brian gave us that bass harmony while Nicky sang melody brilliantly. We just couldn't decide between them, so Louis suddenly said, 'Well, why don't we have both of them?'

Someone pointed out that we'd then be back to six members.

'Well, in that case,' said Louis, 'we'll include them both and take a vote on the final five.'

I spoke to Nicky and said, 'What we want to do to make up our mind is this: will you come down to Sligo with Brian and live with us for a while? We'll rehearse, hang out, get to know each other better. Then we'll take a vote on the final five.'

He didn't know us at all and I know he'd been with Georgina three years at this stage, but he was very keen. He said yes, and so did Brian.

It's interesting, looking back, because Louis really let us pick to a certain extent. He gave us a lot of power in that decision. I know why too. Louis had done the Boyzone thing and that was a band that had come together for the project. We were a band that had already started and had this tight camaraderie; we were proper mates. Louis liked that. He didn't want it to be 'his' band, he wanted it to be 'our' band. He thought that was a better way of approaching it.

So I come back home to me mam and dad's, *explains Nicky*, and tell them that I'm now going to move to Sligo to live with an unsigned boy band. I remember my mam's face. I could sense she was thinking, *What are you doing now, love?*

I got the train down there with Brian. It was quite awkward, because they sent me to live with Michael at his parents' house and Brian went to stay with Shane. I'd heard that Louis was quite keen to get rid of Michael, so I felt very uncomfortable sleeping under his roof, if that was the case. I remember standing outside his sitting room and he was talking to his parents, explaining about these two Dublin boys and what was going to happen. Then I heard his mum say, 'Well, are they any good?' You could tell alarm bells were ringing for her. To be fair, Michael said, 'Yes, they are both very good.'

We all went out for a beer that night and I told Shane it was just too uncomfortable, it didn't feel right being at Michael's. He was really cool about it and afterwards made up some reason why it would be easier for me to stay over at his parents' café.

Louis had said to the lads, 'I'm not making that call from six to five, because I've already got rid of Derek and Graham.' People might think Louis is a cut-throat music biz manager, but he isn't like that. Because of the family connection with Shane's mum in Kiltimagh, I don't think he felt comfortable being that harsh with them. That's why he said it had to go to a vote. He did have a vote himself, but it was only one of five. He had always given the band a lot of power, which was fantastic for me to see, coming from football, where you were given none.

In the meantime, *continues Kian*, Louis had organized several showcases for UK record labels and people were flying in to see us. We rehearsed for several weeks and got really tight. Then we all swapped places and left Sligo to live with Brian and Nicky in Dublin (Mark stayed with his aunty in Black Rock).

The label Louis really wanted this time around was Virgin. The Spice Girls were massive at the time with them and on the day we auditioned for them, their act Billie Piper had gone to number 1 and Louis was dead set on getting them.

Michael knew he was under pressure and at that audition he'd pulled a chair up beside the two girls from Virgin and was being really friendly, talking about the Spice Girls and all that. I think perhaps he sold himself a bit too much, though. It was awkward to see, but to be fair he wanted to impress, he knew the pressure was on.

At one point, Louis took Michael to one side and used one of his all-time favourite sayings: 'Michael, you're trying too hard.'

We did an entire dance routine, *says Shane*, and then five *a capella* songs, and I think we sang it all very well.

They didn't like us.

Louis was gutted.

We couldn't believe it, because we were really confident in what we were doing and in our ability. It really bothered Louis.

Although I'd heard I had a good chance, *recalls Nicky*, and that Michael's position was weak, I was still very nervous when the day came to take a vote on the final five members of the band. We met at the Red Box and all went to a room where Louis was waiting for us. He announced that there was to be a vote to decide which one out of three lads were going to get cut.

'It's between Nicky, Michael and Brian,' he said.

We were all sitting round a circular table and it was pretty tense. I would imagine Kian, Mark and Shane were pretty relieved, although it had been fairly common knowledge that they were going to be safe.

Graham, who'd been in the band but then been cut and made tour manager, said, 'Right, the majority want Brian to be in the band at the moment.'

I kind of knew this was the way it was heading, so now it was down to just me and Michael. Still, I was devastated. Michael was too, he just put his head down. I was looking around nervously, unsure what to think. Shane had spoken to me previously and pretty much said Louis had an issue with Michael but here we were, nonetheless ...

Louis said, 'I'll leave it up to you, I don't want to make this call, lads.'

Michael never moved. His head was still bowed.

So Graham said, 'We are going to have a secret ballot in the toilet ...' and as he was talking, Louis Walsh was looking at me, sticking his thumb up and pointing at me.

We all voted and then Graham, God bless him, came out with the bits of paper. He stood at the table and then spoke: 'The members of IOYOU are: Shane Filan, Kian Egan, Mark Feehily, Brian McFadden and Nicky Byrne.'

Michael just sank. His shoulders fell, he was devastated. Then his phone rang and he just threw it across the room and walked away from the table. Some of the lads went to give him a pat on the back and talk to him, but he was too upset, he wasn't really having any of it.

I went over and said, 'Look, Michael, I'm probably the last person you want to hear say this, but I got a proper kick in the bollocks when I left Leeds. You've just got to pick yourself up and move on.'

He didn't even acknowledge me. I don't blame him, to be fair – it was a really hard situation to be in.

The atmosphere was really sombre and although I was delighted, it didn't feel right to jump up and down and shout and all that. I shook all the lads' hands and they congratulated me. Then I made for the door.

I opened it and there was Louis Walsh, grinning from ear to ear like an excited schoolboy, holding his mobile phone towards me, saying, 'Ring your mother, ring your mother!'

It was so hard for Michael, *reflects Shane*. It was difficult for us, but I can't imagine how gutted he must have been. It was so harsh on him.

At the time, Gillian's best friend Helena was dating Michael and the girls had been on a two-week holiday to America together. So Michael and myself went off to the airport to pick them up and it was so weird, so uncomfortable, like. Poor Nicky was the driver! I was meeting my girlfriend and I was in the band; Michael was meeting his girlfriend and he wasn't. It was terrible. He was crying, he was so disappointed, and I can totally understand that.

Michael was a good-looking lad, he was a sound man, he was great, but he probably had the weakest voice out of all of us. We knew it and maybe Michael knew it too. His personality was great – he was a cracking fella – but it came down to him and it was terrible again.

Michael went on to become a copper in Ireland, *says Nicky*, which was ironic for me. I'd done my school exams and then some exams for the Irish police force, the Gardaí, and I was waiting on a medical to be called when I was chosen to be in IOYOU. My mam got a letter not long afterwards giving me a date for my Garda medical and a start day for training. She wrote back and said I was 'otherwise engaged'.

Thank you for your
Support, it means
everything!

MARK

CHAPTER SEVEN

THE POWER OF LOUIS WALSH

L ouis started phoning me to talk about the band, *explains Kian*, and I would then relay the information on to the rest of the boys. It saved him making five identical calls, I suppose, and I was always very excitable, enthusiastic. I would give him an opinion and be keen to go and tell all the lads whatever the news was. I think he got a buzz off that.

I would never have spoken back to him in a million years. That was Louis Walsh on the telephone to me, here, whatever he says is God, because he'd made the biggest boy band in Ireland.

Louis Walsh is an A+ in music, he knows every song that's ever been written. That man's a walking encyclopaedia of music.

Minutes after Simon Cowell had left the first audition, *recalls Shane*, when I'd been drunk the night before and performed so badly, Louis took me to one side and said, 'Listen, dye your hair blond for the next time Cowell comes.'

'What?'

'Dye your hair blond, then he won't recognize you.'

'Are you serious?' I asked.

'Absolutely. Shane, he auditions dozens of people every week. He saw you for about five minutes. He's not going to remember you.'

He was serious.

The next audition for Simon, we actually had mics and backing tracks, *says Mark*. We'd even got a stylist, a local Dublin woman, who'd made us look like characters out of Grand Theft Auto! This was back in the day when we didn't really know what style we were going to be. I remember Louis saying he wanted us to be a male All Saints.

So the day came when we were due to perform for Simon, *continues Kian*, this time with the full latterday Westlife line-up: Shane, Nicky, Brian, me and Mark. It was in the Pod nightclub, so at least it was a bit bigger than the last audition. Shane's hair was longer and blond, as per Louis' cunning plan, and he'd been on a couple of sunbeds so he was browner. As we were about to start, Simon pointed at Shane and said to Louis – I swear to God – 'Who's the new guy?'

Louis came over to us, laughing quietly, and said to Shane, 'He hasn't got a clue who you are. It's worked – he thinks Nicky, Brian and you are the new boys ... And I'm not going tell him either.'

We were all extremely rehearsed and ready for this.

The first song was called 'Everybody Knows', a really strong ballad. We started it and immediately we were on top form, the harmonies were superb, we nailed it.

MARK xx

Probably begging for something!

I obviously got what I wanted!

On my dad's shoulders at the St Patrick's Day Parade, 1981. This picture was on the front page of the local paper.

Fond memories – me with my cousins at Nana Feehily's.

A trip to Westport House with Dad and my brother Barry.

Dancing with Mum at a family gathering.

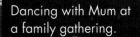

Barry's second birthday party at Nana Verdon's.

My first Holy Communion. I think I made £164.

Nicky

below The first ever photograph of me.

Me and my sister Gillian on her first day at school.

Practising the 'Nicky look' at an early age.

Me with Adzer, an amazing surprise to get a new little brother.

Mam was my first ever stylist.

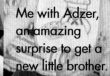

Meet the parents – six years before little Adam joined us.

Pontins winner

I should have won 'Worst Haircut'.

My late Nana Byrne.

'Best Goalkeepr in Europe', aged 12, 1990.

Italia '90.

Living the pop star life already, aged 10.

Front row, far left, Leeds United F.C.

My first year at school.

Me aged 3 with my sister, Mairead, outside the Carlton Café.

My first trip to England on a boat, with Dad, aged 3.

With my three brothers, Finbarr, Peter and Liam, at the All Ireland Minor Hurling Finals at Croke Park, aged 7.

My Confirmation Day aged 11.

At a family Holy Communion.

Left–right: Dad, me, and my brothers Peter and Finbc

Out for dinner with Mairead, Liam and Denise.

Me and my older brother Tom.

My baby brother Colm with my first guitar.

Left–right: Tom, David Dolan, myself and David McGowan. The young crew of Lynndale.

My first Holy Communion.
Left–right: Grandmother Rose, my mum, my sister Fenella and Dad.

They wished they'd never bought me this after a few hours!

Winning my first prize at the feis, despite an ear infection.

Me and Graham in my bedroom.

Only 30 seconds into that first song we noticed Simon leaning over to Louis and whispering something into his ear.

Later on, we found out what he'd said.

'Louis, I'll sign them.'

Although Simon told Louis he'd sign us after 30 seconds, *says Shane*, we carried on and sang about six songs, some Boyzone, some Boyz II Men and some Backstreet Boys tunes. We were half-singing, half-watching Simon, who was nodding with an approving look on his face, *exactly* as you now see him do on *X Factor*. Remember, we didn't know he'd already said he'd sign us, so I was just seeing this and thinking, *I don't reckon he thinks we're shite* ...

Afterwards, he came and sat down with us.

'I really like you guys. You've got great looks, good harmonies. You're a bit unique. You're not like Boyzone and you're not like the Backstreet Boys, I see you as a genuine male vocal pop group.'

He liked the combination of my vocal with Mark's − mine is a more pop voice, it has an edgier tone, while Mark's has that incredible R&B vibe to it, not what you'd expect from a white Irish kid − and he loved Kian, Nicky and Brian's melodies and harmonies.

We liked the idea of being a male vocal group; we knew we weren't brilliant dancers so we didn't want to be jumping round the place doing body rolls. It was more about the vocal for us, and he'd already kinda seen what we wanted to be. He was saying all the right things as far as we were concerned.

Then he started talking about songwriters and producers he was thinking of, *explains Kian*, people like Max Martin, Steve Mac,

Wayne Hector, all these massive songwriters who'd had huge hits for massive bands.

As soon as he'd left, Louis came bouncing over.

'He loved you guys! He wants to sign you! You were all brilliant!' He was so excited. 'Simon's the one I wanted to sign you, he's the man that will make what I want to happen with you happen.'

We totally put our trust in Louis.

He knew Simon Cowell was the right man to go with.

The main reason I really committed to doing the band, *says Nicky,* was because Louis was behind it and we all knew what he'd done with Boyzone. I'm not saying I wouldn't have done it without Louis being involved, but I'd have been far more sceptical. It just always felt like it was going to work with him involved. One thing about Louis that people don't realize is he does it because he *loves* it – he wouldn't do it for free, of course, but he doesn't do it for the money. So when he said Cowell was the man for the job, we trusted him.

Mark continues, Shortly after that, they wanted to get us in the studio. I knew Cowell liked my voice and Shane's a lot, but the next step was to see if our live voices worked as well on tape, because that's not always the case – as Cowell says on *American Idol* a lot, you may not have a 'recording voice'. So they flew me and Shane to Sweden to make a few samplers. They must have liked what they heard, because the record label Simon Cowell worked for, Sony-BMG, soon confirmed they were offering us a major five-album record deal.

*   *   *

Kian: While the lawyers got busy, Louis pulled two masterstrokes. We were all still in Sligo and Dublin at this point, so we had to live out of suitcases while this was all being sorted out. What we didn't know is that those same suitcases would soon be our way of life. We had no money, so I think Louis paid for a lot of the expenses for us.

One day Louis gave us all £500 each to go and get some new clothes for an important photo shoot we had coming up in the *Evening Herald*. That was great fun; it seemed like so much money. He'd also got us a photo shoot for Levis and we got a pair of free jeans each. Already the papers were talking about us as 'the new Boyzone', so it was a very exciting time.

Louis had kept dropping hints that he wanted Ronan Keating involved in the management side of the band, *explains Shane*. He and Louis were tight, really close, and Ronan came to see us rehearse and really liked us. Why wouldn't we want Ronan involved? He was a superstar! So eventually we went to a meeting with him. He was a total gentleman. He offered us some advice and then it was agreed that it would be announced that he was our co-manager. Ronan received half of the management commission, but it was a stroke of genius by yer man Louis Walsh. It created such a buzz around the band, it was a very clever publicity stunt, and we benefited from it hugely.

You've got to hand it to Louis, *agrees Nicky*, it was a masterstroke announcing Ronan was co-manager. Obviously, Ronan didn't do the majority of the day-to-day managing; he was never going to, that was Louis. But the impact that had within Boyzone fan circles was huge.

Louis wasn't afraid to play up to 'the new Boyzone' tag. He explained to us that when that band had first started, they had hogged Take That gigs in Dublin. They had literally stood outside with photos of themselves, meeting the Take That fans going in, chatting to them, charming them and telling them all about their new band. So, when Boyzone were massive, we did the very same thing, standing outside handing out leaflets and walking up and down the queue until the doors were opened. Very cleverly, Louis and Sony-BMG had these business cards printed with Ronan's details on there as co-manager. The girls would stop and chat and we'd give them our little card, saying we were going to be the next big boy band and, pretty soon, we were having pictures taken with these fans. Of course, if they saw Ronan's name on the card, that made a huge difference. It was hard graft, but we loved it. You have to be into what you do and we loved it. We worked our asses off to be in with a chance.

Let me tell you about a funny incident during these early days. We were staying at Castle Leslie, County Monaghan, and it was supposed to be haunted. We all had a few drinks then went back to our rooms for some kip. Now we'd already had the hotel tour and they'd said some rooms were more haunted than others. We were all shiteing ourselves, I'm telling you.

Before Shane got to his room, I slipped in there and hid in a chest at the base of his bed. I must have had to wait about 20 minutes – I kept lifting the lid up and going, *Where the fuck is he?* – before I finally heard the door handle turn and Shane come in. I peeped out from under the lid, and he was just kind of looking around the room. You could see he was uneasy. Then I just jumped out and went 'Aaarrrggghhh!!'

He fell to the floor, shit himself and then he went after me! He didn't do anything, obviously, but he was furious.

Then he said the funniest thing: 'Nicky, you bastard, I could have had a stroke!'

That comment made me laugh even more. I was pissing myself – he was only 19, and he was saying he could have had a stroke!

Yeah, *says Shane*, I was fuming. I nearly killed him I did, I could have strangled him there and then! I said sorry, like ... Fucker!

Before Louis pulled his second masterstroke, we changed our name, *continues Kian*. Simon thought IOYOU was wrong. 'If I'm being perfectly honest,' he said, 'it's terrible, absolutely terrible.' He suggested the name Westside, as he felt it fitted our west of Ireland roots.

Then Louis told us that we would be going on tour with Boyzone. We were so excited.

So excited, we almost died! *says Shane*. Well, not exactly, but on the way up to their Belfast show, I thought my end had come. Mark's dad Ollie was driving us up from Sligo – me, Mark and Kian – and there'd been some really icy weather. The road was black with ice; it was awful. The road out of Sligo towards Belfast isn't the best – it's very windy and narrow – and we were slipping and skidding all over the place. There was nothing Ollie could do about it, it was like an ice-skating rink. We were laughing at first because it was comical, the car having a mind of its own. Then there was one particular corner that we skidded towards with a vertical drop of about 100 feet the other side, and we weren't laughing then. I really thought my time was up. I remember thinking, *Aaahh! I'm not gonna get to support Boyzone! Aaahh!*

We ended up driving at about 15 mph and I thought we were going to die on at least 25 separate occasions! It took over six hours to get there – the longest six hours of my life.

Going on tour with Boyzone in all these massive arenas was insane, *recalls Mark.* Even though they weren't always full to capacity when we sang, it was *brilliant.* We did some shows with Boyzone in Europe, quite a few in the UK and then it sort of intertwined with a *Smash Hits* tour as well.

That was when it started to sink in that I wasn't going to be able to pop back home to Sligo all the time. I remember asking one of the girls out of B*Witched when they'd last been home and she said, 'Two months.' That was a real reality check. But although that worried me, I was having a great time.

There we were, on tour supporting Boyzone without a record deal, *says Kian.* Next thing we know, we were on the big Saturday TV show *CD:UK* without a record deal. Next thing up, we got a slot playing on the *Smash Hits Roadshow,* which then led to us winning a *Smash Hits* award for Best New Touring Act – the power of Louis Walsh.

Mark: I remember an incident with Louis way back then that showed me how serious he was about his bands being totally professional. We were doing a TV appearance in Ireland and there was another Irish boy band in the green room beforehand, getting a bit lairy and drunk. They weren't terrible, but they were having a few.

Louis was standing next to us and he said, 'If I ever see you doing that, I'll leave in a second. If I see you hanging around in the green room drinking beer before you go on TV, I'm finished.'

*   *   *

Signing the actual record contract was amazing, *recounts Nicky*. It was in the first week of November 1998, while we were still on tour with Boyzone. A lot of the lads hadn't even been to London before; I was a little more experienced in that I'd been to America, Canada and much of Europe with family holidays and football tournaments.

Louis was travelling to the record label seperately, so it was literally the five of us travelling over on a plane to meet him there. We made our way from the airport to this big office block where the record company was based. I remember that standing there, ready to go in, we were just giddy kids. Looking back, as soon as we entered that doorway, all of our lives changed beyond recognition.

We went into a big meeting room that is now Simon Cowell's private office but back then was just a huge conference room. Sonny Takhar was also there, Simon's right-hand man who has also been instrumental in our career.

We knew it was a big record deal – we signed for five albums on a contract worth several million pounds, so, understandably at that age, we all thought that once we'd signed this piece of paper, we'd be millionaires. Of course that money is split over the albums and it has to go towards paying for some incredibly expensive stuff like accommodation, clothes, cars, video shoots, recording costs and so on. It's funny, looking back, because we'd all been looking at what cars we could afford. Rather than get proper carried away, I was thinking of buying maybe a Toyota MR2, you know, for 15 grand, say – nothing too ridiculous. That's how you think at that age.

Signing that record deal was all my dreams come true, *says Kian*. It really was a lifelong dream and here we were, signing the contract, about to record an album, put singles out, travel the world in a band and make music. It was just *amazing*.

It was the stuff of dreams, absolutely, *recalls Shane*. All my life I'd been looking forward to this moment. It was one of my major goals in life, but I never thought it would happen. I knew I wanted to get married and I hoped I'd be a father, but I never thought I'd get a massive record deal. It's such a prized achievement for a band.

I can't really ever forget that excitement, that moment sitting in that office, all the thoughts buzzing around my head: *We are going to be pop stars! We might have a hit single!* Then the teenage thoughts kick in, like *Maybe I'm going to be a millionaire!* Then, most importantly of all, *I can go and buy a new car!*

Signing the record deal was a huge decision for me, *says Mark*. I can clearly remember actually putting the pen on the page where I was supposed to sign. I can see it now, the pen moving in slow motion as I signed my name.

At that precise second, a thousand thoughts were buzzing through my brain. I was excited about the deal, naturally, but I was *very* nervous about what it meant for my life back in Sligo. I was really scared that it might change things.

Of course it changed everything beyond recognition.

Subconsciously, I must have known this and that is why signing that piece of paper was such a big deal for me. There I was, an 18-year-old country boy, flying into this big corporate office in the middle of London, being surrounded by all these big names in the business, working for this worldwide company, sitting by accountants, lawyers, managers – it felt insane. I think in the back of my mind I'd been preparing to go to college, like a lot of kids do from around Sligo, then suddenly here I was signing a multi-million pound record deal with all the heavy responsibility that comes with that. Maybe for a kid brought up in Camden, it would have been an easy day out, but for me the contrast was so severe. Exciting, thrilling, scary, daunting, all at once. I'm just trying to be really honest here.

As I signed, the noise of the city outside was as far from my idyllic country childhood as you can imagine. I could feel that distance sitting there in that room, writing my name on that sheet of paper.

Right there and then, I put a barrier up.

This is not going to change me, this is not going to change my life, I kept saying to myself. It was important at that point to have that feeling. It reassured me. I hadn't travelled like Nicky, I didn't have the confidence of Shane, Kian and Brian. But, ultimately, the draw to sing was greater than the desire for my life not to change, so I signed the contract.

But I just kept telling myself it wouldn't really change anything. How wrong can you be?

The business side of it hit us instantly, *says Nicky*. We had to set up a company, we hired an accountant, Alan McEvoy, and we got lawyers and tour managers lined up, all sorts. It was explained to us that the company, Blue Net, should own the band name because if any member were to leave then the band could continue without legal problems. We just agreed – it sounded reasonable and besides, no one was going to leave Westlife, were they?

As soon as we signed the deal, we spoke with Louis and he said, 'Right, you're going straight into a recording studio.'

Game on.

PART II

CHAPTER EIGHT

THE FIRST OF MANY

From the phone call in the pub from Louis, saying he'd got us a slot supporting the Backstreet Boys, *remembers Shane*, to our first single, which was released in April 1999, it was just 13 months. The pace of it all was insane. And it was about to get much more insane ...

Next thing we know, *says Nicky*, we're on a plane to Sweden to begin recording our debut album. It was moving so fast. It seemed that even before the ink was dry on the record contract, the pace of our lives flipped to light-speed.

There was one more name change to come: we discovered that there were several overseas acts already using the name Westside, so we altered it once again, this time to Westlife. It was between this and West High, which I preferred, but all the other lads wanted Westlife.

We made our way to the Cheiron studio, all incredibly excited. All the big American pop bands recorded at that place in Sweden.

The Backstreet Boys had been there a week before we flew out for the debut album sessions. Fans would circle around the reception and entrance to the studio and when we walked out they'd be like, 'Who are you?!' But instead of laughing or taking offence, we would introduce ourselves and tell them we were Westlife, what we were doing and that we were going to be a big new boy band, and that's how we started building up our fanbase.

Other than that, I remember those first album sessions to be full of sickness. It was freezing cold in Stockholm, absolutely bitter, and in fact I got so sick I was eventually flown home.

Our first single was to be a song called 'Swear It Again' and it was due for release in late April 1999. I remember that earlier Shane came back to the house we were all staying at in Dublin and excitedly played us this demo. It was a version of 'Swear It Again' sung by session vocalists. I think it was maybe even Mac's co-writer, Wayne Hector, singing. I distinctly remember thinking, *Wow, this is a great song. It's a big chorus, great harmonies. This is exactly what we want to be recording.*

We shot the video for 'Swear It Again', *explains Kian*, and Cowell *hated* it, he tore it to pieces. He'd spent £150,000 on it and he just threw it in the bin. We reshot the video completely and did five or six different photo shoots with five or six different stylists. It was really a case of no expense spared by Simon and the label.

Between them, Simon and Louis got us on all the front covers of magazines before we'd even released a single. We were the first band to ever be on the front cover of *Smash Hits* without releasing a single.

In the lead-up to the single's release, *remembers Shane*, we were hearing good things from the record company. Radio was loving it, the record shops were ordering good numbers of copies ... It sounded good to us, but to be fair, we had never done it before, so we actually had no idea what it all meant.

As the week of release approached, they kept saying, 'Lads, it's going to be a big song.' They told us that all the signs were there for a Top Ten. Top Ten! We thought this was brilliant. We'd have taken number 10 any day of the week.

Then it came to the actual week of release and we were all sitting in Peter Waterman's studio doing more work on the debut album.

The phone rang and it was Louis with the update.

'Lads, you're going to be number 1.'

It was incredible. We couldn't believe what we were hearing. We were jumping up and down, hugging each other, shouting, just hysterically happy. Pete Waterman came down with a bottle of champagne. It was mental. When we finally heard the official charts and we were indeed on top, I know this sounds silly now, but I remember looking out of the window and pointing at all the streets, going, 'We're number 1 there, there ... and there ... and there!'

It got better. 'Swear It Again' stayed at number 1 for the next week too.

We got to do *Top of the Pops* two weeks running, which was brilliant, a dream come true. It was a fairytale. I don't want to sound clichéd, but it literally was the stuff dreams are made of.

Within just over 12 months, our lives had been totally turned upside down. We'd wanted to be a famous band, we'd wanted a record deal, we'd wanted to be number 1, and now it had all happened. And it had happened so *fast*. From being six in the band to being five, to meeting Simon, signing the record deal, officially becoming Westlife, recording a single and then hitting number 1, it was a year and two weeks – as quick as that.

Unbelievable.

The single didn't stop there either – it was a massive hit all around the world.

Suddenly, everyone was talking about Westlife.

From that moment, it was pure insanity, *says Kian*. We were in Tenerife a week later shooting a video for our second single, 'If I Let You Go', and then we came back and released that and it went to number 1 as well. Then we went to Mexico to shoot another video and in between all this we were doing all the TV shows, promo in and out of Europe and the Far East, and flying everywhere, just go, go, go, go, go!

That opening single started a record-breaking run of singles going in at number 1. It stretched from April 1999 to November 2000, when our seventh single, 'My Love', hit the top spot. It was only with our eighth single, 'What Makes a Man', and a certain kids' TV character, that we failed to enter straight at the top. But we'll come to that.

For now, it was sheer pandemonium. After our second single had gone straight to the top, next up came one of Westlife's biggest ever songs: 'Flying without Wings'. There's a story to tell behind that massive track.

We've always enjoyed a great relationship with Simon Cowell, *explains Nicky*. Back in the day, before *X Factor* and *American Idol*, before he became a huge celebrity, he was an A&R man at a record company working 9 to 5 (and then some). At that point, when he was intimately involved, there was no one to touch him. He'd call you up on your mobile out of the blue and say, 'Nicky, I just didn't like what you were wearing on *GMTV* today, have a word with the boys.' He'd also call the other lads at times and say stuff like 'You looked tired, you looked overweight, you seemed uninterested' and so on. That might sound negative, but what he was very clever at was making you all feel special, because he'd comment on your performance or appearance in a way that was *constructive*. It was more of an observation than a criticism. We knew he was trying to get the band to sound its best, look its best, perform at its best.

You'd sit in a meeting and I noticed after a while that during the course of the discussion he'd make direct eye contact with every single one of us, or maybe give a nod, a look or a friendly wink to each of us. No one felt left out. In complete contrast to the public perception of 'Nasty' Simon Cowell, he's an expert at making people feel special.

He was the character with the high waist-band and low-necked T-shirt, *says Kian*. You know, 'Darling, look …' We used to rip the piss out of him, we'd sit in meetings and just be like, 'Love the shoes, Simon. Love the trousers. D'ya want to pull them up a wee bit higher?' But do you know what? He's not wrong very often. If you're like me, you'll sit there and watch these talent shows where he's knocking people, and if the truth is known, it's what most of us are thinking.

In terms of being your A&R man, which is, after all, what our relationship with him is, I think he gets what people like. That's the only way I can describe it: he *gets* what people like. We wanted to learn and I think he taught us well. Without him, we wouldn't be Westlife and we wouldn't be where we are today, in my opinion.

In those very early days, and I'm being very honest here, we were, 'What do you want us to do? Yes, sir, no, sir, three bags full, sir.' That sounds terrible, but actually we *liked* what they were suggesting. We weren't puppets who did stuff against our wishes, we *wanted* to do these things, so it was a happy partnership. Later, we wanted more involvement in all sorts of decisions, of course. I guess that's natural, but at first that's how it was.

Simon is a perfectionist. If he doesn't like a video when he sees the final clip, he'll just say, 'Reshoot it,' almost regardless of cost, just as he did with 'Swear It Again' and has done many times since. One time we did a big awards ceremony and he'd asked one of the stylists not to glisten us up with loads of glitter and stuff. He did, so Simon sacked him the next day.

He knows how to get people excited and interested and involved and to make an idea feel like their baby. He has the amazing power to sit in that office and make you feel like you are *the* man, and then you walk out of there and do it the way he wants it done! He is a clever, clever man. We've gone into so many meetings with Simon saying, 'Right, we can't let him do that to us again,' and 30 minutes later, he's won us round yet again.

Back then, we knew that he was a big hitter, *says Shane.* There's a famous music business story that shows the lengths Simon will go to for his artists. As we were starting our careers, his boy band Five were very big news. Simon had heard of a song written by the pop songwriting legend Max Martin, who has penned tracks for the likes of the Backstreet Boys, N*Sync and latterly Kelly Clarkson. It was a track called 'Hit Me Baby, One More Time'. We all know this now, of course, as Britney Spears's breakthrough tune, a very famous pop song. But back then, Simon wanted it for Five. The rumour went that he was so keen to get it that he even offered Max Martin a Ferrari.

Max didn't take the gift and didn't give Five the song, but it shows you how passionate Cowell is about getting the right songs for his artists. We knew that he knew he would get us the songs we needed to make it big.

And when he heard 'Flying without Wings', he had to have it for Westlife.

So he did, simple as that.

We first heard the song in demo form in a meeting with Simon, Sonny, Steve Mac, his co-writer Wayne Hector and Louis. It was obviously a great tune, even in that early form. We'd heard that several singers were after it, including, I believe, Stephen Gateley. Steve Mac knew the potential Westlife had at this point – we had become *massive* within just a few months of 1999, so he could see the sense in giving it to us. It must have felt good for him to sit there with that monster song up his sleeve.

Simon made all sorts of fantastic offers to secure this song. I think it was part of the package that Steve and Wayne were made executive producers on the album alongside himself, not least because so many of their tunes were on the album. Thankfully, they chose to let us record it and in doing so gave us one of our signature tracks.

In the early days, that song presented me with a little bit of an issue, *recalls Mark*. There's a part in 'Flying without Wings' which everyone calls 'the high note'. It's not actually that high, but everyone goes on about it. For the longest time when we were singing it live, I'd be like, *Oh, here comes that bastard note, I'm going to have to try and hit it and everyone is waiting to see if I can do it live and ... here we go, here we go ... here it comes ...*

It was becoming a real issue, even though I knew I could hit this note in my sleep. Eventually, Shane sat me down to talk about it. He just said, 'Stop thinking about it, just shout it out and who cares if you fluff it, whatever.' He was so confident about it, so practical, it was brilliant advice. It was only after I stopped worrying about that note that I was able to sing it properly on stage.

It's probably fair to say I sometimes suffer lows more than I enjoy highs. When something good happens, I think, *Great*, and move on quite quickly, but if something bad happens, I tend to dwell on it. I don't actually think that's a bad thing, though, especially when you're talking about singing, because it drives you on to be good and keeps you on your toes.

Shane: 'Flying without Wings' sold 350,000 copies on its way to number 1 and was a massive international hit. It was on the radio everywhere. A sign of how it is now seen as a pop classic is that when we released a live version in 2004, it became the first ever download number 1 nearly five years after its original release. Perhaps most importantly for us at the time, 'Flying without Wings' was a definite turning-point in our career. It took us from being seen as a pop boy band to a vocal group.

*   *   *

Before our next single, we released our self-titled debut album in November 1999, *Shane continues*. By this point, Ronan had stepped away from the management side of Westlife. He was a great adviser and a good friend, but he was happy to move away now we'd become a big concern.

One of the biggest misconceptions about Westlife, *explains Nicky*, is that we are a covers band. Our first three singles were originals. The first cover we did was the double A-side 'I Have a Dream/Seasons in the Sun' in December 1999. It felt right to do a cover at that point, because Christmas is that type of market. That release went straight in at number 1 again, the fourth time we'd done this. Plus, it kept selling for several weeks after Christmas, making it the last number 1 of the old century and the first number 1 of the new millennium.

Just before this, we were nominated for Record of the Year for 'Flying without Wings' ... We couldn't believe it.

We were in ridiculously high-profile company: Ronan Keating had 'When You Say Nothing at All', and Shania Twain was also nominated; it was mad. We thought we had no chance of winning the thing, we were just naïve and very excited to have been nominated. To be totally honest, we assumed we were there to make up the numbers and have a piss-up.

As long as we don't come last ...

We performed the song and Simon Cowell and Sonny Takhar were really on the ball, as always. They put us on stage with a gospel choir and a beautiful set, no expense spared.

Then, when everyone had performed, the vote counting began in the various regional centres, much like on Eurovision. At first, Ronan and Britney were streets ahead and we were down in fifth, still happy to be there, still happy to be having a piss-up. Just happy to get some free drinks, really ... *As long as we don't come last* ...

Then we went to Northern Ireland and we cleaned up.

Then we went around parts of the north and were cleaning up again. Suddenly, we weren't fifth, we were fourth, then third, then second. Manchester loved us, so did Newcastle, *and* we were drinking free beer. It was great craic.

Then, bang, we were in first place and it was all over.

We'd won Record of the Year.

We've won it a further three times since.

I know Ronan well now and I still take the piss out of him about this first win, but to be fair, he must have been gutted.

We couldn't believe it. Brian picked Denise van Outen up on his shoulders and spun her around when she handed us the trophy. I was made up. I love winning trophies. I'm very competitive – it doesn't matter if it's a game of tiddly winks or an arm wrestle or football or PlayStation. The lads will tell you. I remember winning Best Goalkeeper at quite an important European tournament for the Home Farm team in Dublin, and I have a picture of me and my parents at Dublin airport, hugging and holding on to the trophy like it was the World Cup. So to win something like this with Westlife was amazing.

Brian gave me the trophy, a lovely gold statue of a woman holding a glass record aloft above her slender shoulders.

We had to sing the song again, then as soon as we'd finished, I jumped off the stage and ran over to Steve Mac and Wayne Hector, who'd written the winning song.

I threw my arms around Steve and smashed the trophy in half across his back.

I'd only had the thing five minutes.

When we went home that first Christmas, we realized our lives had changed forever, *continues Nicky*. I walked home, went to the local pub for Christmas Eve, and bang, it literally hit me. Let me explain.

I had this thing with my mates which dated back to when I was 16, coming back from Leeds and wanting to make sure I saw them all at Christmas time. We'd all go for a pint at the local and have a laugh. This Christmas Eve, I noticed straight away I was getting a lot of attention.

I was with the lads in the International Bar in Dublin and we were actually starting to think about going home when this girl came up to me. She had a tattoo on her arm, but it was one of those that looked very DIY, home-made even. It was pretty rough. Some of the letters looked blurred, a bit scribbled out, so one of my mates, just being cheeky, having a laugh and said, 'Did you not like your tattoo? Why don't you get some Tippex?' This girl took offence, but instead of answering back to my mate, she turned around and slapped me!

In the early days, we used to get a fair bit of verbal too. Blokes on the street would shout 'Queers!', all that sort of crap. At first, you're a bit taken aback, but you get used to it and, to be fair, it doesn't happen anymore.

One time we were doing a photo shoot on an open-topped bus in Dublin and it was attracting quite a bit of attention. We stopped at some traffic lights and a white Transit van pulled up alongside us. The bloke driving it looked up at us, all dressed immaculately for the shoot, shouted, 'Westlife! Arse bandits!' and drove off.

We fell about laughing. Not a lot you can say to that, is there?!

CHAPTER NINE

BUZZING WITH THE QUEEN BEE

W e need to make one thing perfectly clear, *explains Mark*. We never agreed to be 'single' or 'available'. Nicky had been with Georgina for some time, likewise Shane with Gillian.

Gillian was going to college at the time, *recounts Shane*, and was very keen not to have Westlife affect that. She wanted a normal college life. As I remember it, no one ever said to us, 'You can't have a girlfriend.' If they'd have said that was essential it would have been the end of the band, like. Without a doubt, because for me I wanted Gillian in my life above everything else.

It was her idea really, not to publicize it so much. She wanted her own friends, her own time at college. Her best friends knew, obviously, but she didn't just want to be the girl who was going out with the guy in Westlife. Later on, people started realizing, but by then she'd managed to enjoy a normal life at college.

Whatever she wanted, I wanted. This was the girl I wanted to spend the rest of my life with, long before Westlife or college or any of this. I loved her then and I just wanted to do whatever she wanted. I knew her personality, what she loved, what she didn't like, her pastimes. Remember, I'd admired her from afar in Sligo and we'd even written a song about her, as you know. I'd been a friend of hers for maybe seven years before we got together.

She *got* Westlife. She understood what it meant – that there'd be attention from girls – and she knew how to handle it all, she had no problem with that. There's no other woman in the world who comes close to her. I'd fallen in love with her and that was that. So the band situation really didn't affect us, to be honest.

From Day One, Nicky was known to be going out with the Taoiseach's daughter, *says Kian*. He never kept it a secret, never discussed saying otherwise. It was as simple as that. Even when he auditioned, next to his picture it stated who he was dating. He never went out the back door of a nightclub with Georgina to keep it quiet. We've always been adamant that's one thing we're not going to bluff anyone about. If someone had said to us, 'You all have to be single and available,' I'm convinced we would have said, 'Shove your contract.'

I seem to remember Louis saying something about us not publicizing any girlfriends, though. He didn't say we couldn't have any, it was more about not making a big public show of them.

It didn't bother me one way or the other, to be honest with you. I had a few girlfriends here and there, nothing too serious. I wasn't about to run off and get married. I know Nicky and Shane had different situations, but for me it wasn't really a big deal.

Louis leaked stories at the beginning that I was going out with Bertie Ahern's daughter, *says Nicky*, because it was a huge story in Ireland, so it was another spin for him at the beginning when Westlife needed press. I didn't really mind either way. I'd found somebody that I loved and wanted to spend the rest of my life with and that was it. It was perfect for me that Georgina's dad was in the public eye, because the record company couldn't ignore that fact, so I didn't have to hide her, which I think can be difficult. There was never a question of 'I can't have a girlfriend,' it was more a question of 'How do I make everything in my life balanced?' First and foremost I wanted my girlfriend to be my wife and then I wanted my career to be the biggest it could be.

*   *   *

We didn't tour the first album, *recalls Mark*, so it was straight into summer recording sessions for the follow-up, to be called *Coast to Coast* and set for a November 2000 release.

We'd been nominated for an MTV Award in early 2000 for Best UK and Ireland Act, which was brilliant. And we won. Mariah Carey had also been nominated for an award. We all went down to London for the press call for the nominations and it was a suitably star-studded event. Then I heard someone whisper that Mariah Carey was in the building. I couldn't believe it. I was so excited, I can't tell you. Now, because I listen to so much music and hear so many songs from other artists, Mariah is by no means the only artist in my record collection, but back then she was still someone I'd always wanted to meet.

There we were, standing around backstage waiting for stuff to get started, and then she walked past. My eyes were on stalks. She looked absolutely gorgeous and just floated by. For me, that was a *huge* moment. Here was this woman who had inspired me to start singing seriously, whose voice I'd so admired, whose songs I'd learned every note of – *here she was*, walking past me at an awards press call that my own band was involved in. It was bizarre.

Within about 20 seconds of her walking past, I was scouring the building looking for our record company person, saying, 'Please, this might never happen again, you've got to sort it out so I can say hello to Mariah, please!' Even though I was a huge fan at the time, I was obviously aware of all the rumours that she was supposed to be difficult, a diva, demanding and all that, so I didn't expect much. Also, I was a little concerned that if she was dismissive it would tarnish one of my all-time idols. But at the same time, I had to ask. I thought if I could just say 'Hello' and get a picture, I'd be a happy man.

Then the word came back saying that Mariah would love to meet me.

All the lads were delighted for me and were egging me on. They were brilliant. I followed Mariah's representative down some corridors and finally through a door, then I sort of paused momentarily, aware I was about to meet her. The woman beckoned me through the door ... and I walked into a room packed with media, a full-blown press conference, with Mariah lounging on an extravagant *chaise longue* with 100 flashbulbs taking pictures of her.

This was where they'd arranged for me to meet her, right there and then in front of the assembled press pack. I was too nervous to back out of it, but it was so embarrassing going up onto what was basically a stage with a chair on it and Mariah Carey perched there in front of 100 tabloid journalists.

I introduced myself and said how nice it was to meet her, slightly apprehensive about what she would be like and if she would be mean to me in front of the press. But do you know what? She was lovely. She couldn't have been nicer. She looked me straight in the eye all the time we talked, she gave me her full attention, and she was really kind. I'd managed to get hold of a copy of her album somehow and she signed that and was very gracious about me being a fan. Then suddenly it was all over. I was so pleased she'd been so lovely to me. It was great.

A few weeks later we were in a hotel in South East Asia on a promotional trip, when the door to my room burst open and the rest of the band tumbled in, laughing, shouting, waving and saying, 'Mark! Mark! We're going to do a song with Mariah Carey!' I think they were almost as excited for me as I was myself, which was really nice. They knew how much it meant to me. I don't know how to describe the excitement at hearing that news. It was unreal.

We all knew how much Mark had wanted to meet Mariah properly, *says Nicky*. We knew he had met her previously, albeit briefly. So when we heard about the song with her, we were bursting to tell him. Kian took the call from Louis and I have to admit my exact words when he told me were 'Fuck off, no way!'

It was to be 'Against All Odds', the Phil Collins track, and it would eventually give us our sixth number 1 in 17 months. What's more, we were pencilled in to record the single and video with Mariah in Capri, an island just off Italy.

We had a tiny window of 48 hours to record the single, shoot the video and get it all done.

Kian lost his passport. I felt really sorry for him, because he ended up shooting his parts of the video on his own. Mariah had shot hers on her own, mind you, then we had gone out and done our clips, but because Kian wasn't there, they'd filmed shots of us separately and then spliced it all in later. There were shots of a car with 'Kian' in it, but they were from a distance and cleverly done to hide the fact he wasn't actually there yet and was still desperately trying to get his passport sorted.

We were to have dinner with Mariah in a beautiful Italian restaurant in the most amazing location and we all got there nice and early. The sense of anticipation among the lads was huge. Then suddenly, there she was, like the Queen Bee, gliding in wearing a flowing chiffon outfit. I don't even think her feet were touching the floor, she was gliding that much. It was a real spectacle and obviously everyone in the restaurant was staring at her. She just had that presence. She was probably giving it some for effect, but she definitely had a colossal X factor.

We all sat down and I was trying to eat my pasta but it was just too weird, sitting round a table eating dinner with Mariah Carey. Every now and then I'd relax and chat to one of the lads, then I'd turn my head and think, *Holy shit! That's Mariah Carey!* She was surrounded by 'her people', but actually they kept a distance and let us chat happily with her. I have to say, once we'd got over our nerves, she was an absolute pleasure to talk to. She wasn't at all like the demanding diva you read about in the tabloids.

We shared a beer and had a bit of craic and I even remember, for some reason, that the food was sensational. It was very hard to really be yourself, though. I kept trying to open up and even tell a few jokes, but in the end, I thought, *The less said, the better. You don't want to ruin the night. You don't want Mariah Carey to think you're a knob.*

We hadn't recorded the song at this point, so I think we were all on tenterhooks in case she came away from that meal and said she didn't want to work with us. But that didn't happen, she said she loved our company and I thought she made a huge effort.

Obviously, the best part for me, *recounts Mark*, was singing with Mariah in the studio. I kept thinking back to when I was a kid listening to 'Hero' and all those other great vocals, then pinching myself because I couldn't believe that I was in a studio in Capri with her in person. What's more, she was basically producing us. She had her engineers and all that, but she was sitting behind the desk using the faders and the talk back, telling us to do another take and giving me guidance on a few points. It was incredible.

I have to be honest and say it was actually a bit of a blur! It was all very strange, but good strange, amazing strange. I was really pleased, too, because I wasn't freaking out, I sang my parts calmly and I was proud of them, I wasn't overwhelmed. I was actually very composed and thoroughly enjoying myself. That goes back to what I said about being self-conscious, reserved, anxious to get approval in most parts of my early life except singing, where I just opened my mouth and felt completely liberated. I was definitely a bit nervous, but I realized in those two days that I didn't care who I sang in front of, even Mariah Carey.

And, of course, hearing that voice in person so close was a dream come true.

Personally, I enjoyed the studio time, *continues Nicky*, but I did find it a little intimidating. For a start, there were these three backing singers who were phenomenal, and then you had Mariah Carey, one of the most gifted vocalists in history. The studio was at the top of about 300 stone steps, there was a terrace overhanging a cliff down to the Mediterranean and she had some food brought out for us. It was lovely. I'd set my mind on looking really cool when we first got there, but by the time I'd walked up the 300 steps, I was fucking gasping! It took us like half an hour to get up to the bloody place.

I don't think we had much of a say in any of the video, as she'd decided she wanted her personal videographer to make the clip. We didn't mind – this was Mariah Carey. I definitely don't remember anyone complaining!

Mariah wore a luminous pink dress, and we had to walk along by her. It was surreal – she was walking all light-footed, fluttering her eyelashes at the camera, pure Mariah, and we were all walking alongside, trying to look cool and not look at her and go, 'Jesus, lads, look, Mariah Carey!' I also remember she was brilliantly well lit and we hardly seemed to be lit at all, which made me laugh.

Whatever people say, Mariah was really approachable and although she does that *mwah, mwah, mwah* kissing thing when you meet her, she is genuine and she is always lovely to us whenever we bump into her. It's always, 'Hello again, my Irish boys!'

My favourite story from the various times when we've been lucky enough to meet Mariah has to be when we were all sitting with her after a charity event in Manchester, where we'd sung our duet together. While we were chatting away, from just out of my line of vision a person walked over with a glass of mineral water which had a straw in it. While Mariah was still talking, a hand silently came in from the right and placed the straw directly under her lips. Without even looking at it, Mariah took a few sips from the straw, then the hand silently moved the glass away.

Then another hand, also silently gliding in, came from the left and dabbed the corner of her mouth before sliding away. Mariah was looking straight at me all the time, chatting, and I swear she looked at me with a half-wink, as if to say, *I know you think this is nuts, but this is what I do.* And she did, she had this diva-like presence, this aura, there was certainly none of the unpleasantness that you hear about, nothing at all, and you could see she was playing up to her reputation because it was all part of the show. I smiled about that straw for days.

MARK xx   Kian   Shane   Nicky

CHAPTER TEN

TOO MUCH TORRO ROSSO

*C*oast to Coast was an insane period, *says Kian.* That second album was *huge.* Millions of copies were selling around the world. In the UK, we literally could not walk down the street. Our hotels were mobbed, we were on all the TV shows, all over the radio, the press – it was nuts.

Sonny Takhar had a brilliant idea ahead of the album's release. They hired a private jet, had 'Westlife' splashed down the side and booked in signings in four different cities *in one day.* We were due to visit Glasgow, Manchester, Birmingham and London. The Spice Girls were releasing their 'comeback' album, *Forever*, after Geri Halliwell had left and there was this big chart 'battle' between us and them. So this city-hopping promo jaunt was perfectly designed to ramp up our PR that week. Great idea.

The record label invited a load of media onto the jet to fly around with us – it was great craic. The whole stunt was high profile and we had thousands and thousands of fans turning up in each city. It was insane, proper popstar stuff. There were thousands of people in the streets, they were closing off roads all over the place, the traffic was jammed, it was mental.

I was playing junior-team football at Leeds, *remembers Nicky*, when the Spice Girls were first coming out. All the lads were talking about which Spice Girl they fancied, that was the talk of the football team. They just seemed so famous. Then there I was, in this brilliant band with these brilliant lads, only a few years later, going up against them in a battle of the bands ...

... and beating them hands down, *continues Kian*.

When the charts were announced, we'd creamed the Spice Girls. We'd shifted nearly 250,000 copies and outsold them three to one.

That week was probably the absolute height of Westlife hysteria in the UK. No one could touch us ...

... apart from Bob the Builder, *says Shane*. 'What Makes a Man' was our Christmas single and it was one of our best songs, definitely Top Five Westlife or so. We do it every single year on tour because we still love singing it live so much. It's a cool song – great lyrics and melody, brilliant. So it's a real shame that this was to be our first single that didn't enter at the top.

Those midweek phone calls with our likely chart position were like a ritual by then. And we'd had so many number 1s that there was a burden on us to keep getting the top spot. During the early days, a number 2 became unthinkable.

Oh my God, I couldn't sleep the night before a midweek. I'd be lying in bed at three or four in the morning, thinking about it. Then you'd get the midweek and it would be number 1 and you'd be like, 'Oh, Jesus, the heat's off now ... till the next single.'

That might sound extreme, but we didn't know any different, we *had* to get number 1s. When we beat the Beatles record that was weird enough, but then we got five, six, seven in a row – it was ludicrous.

And then we only hit number 2 with 'What Makes a Man', because of the Bob the Builder Christmas song. The day we found out our midweek, we were gutted. We knew Bob was gonna be big. What was even more frustrating was that it was the biggest first-week sales we'd ever had.

That was such a shock, our first number 2. It was the first time that something hadn't gone perfectly, the first time we'd thought it wasn't all going to be plain sailing.

It was a pity because – I know I'm being greedy now – the next three singles after 'What Makes a Man' also went to number 1, so if Bob hadn't stuck his oar in, we'd have had 11 in a row.

Nevertheless, we're all proud of those seven consecutive number 1 singles, and given the changing climate with downloads and all that, I don't think anyone will ever beat that record. You never know, but it'll be some mighty effort.

*   *   *

We didn't tour the first album, *explains Shane*, which sold 1.5 million copies in the UK alone. Simon Cowell had wanted it this way. Then he didn't want us to tour before the second album. He wanted us to get even bigger first. And he was right. By the time we came to the first headline shows, *Coast to Coast* was selling millions of copies around the world and Westlife was massive.

We set up the 'Where Dreams Come True' world tour.

It was completely sold out within minutes of the tickets going on sale.

That first night in Newcastle was amazing – our first headline arena tour and 11,000 people there, *just* for Westlife.

They'd been waiting two years to see our show. We were a big band and although we'd supported Boyzone at big venues and done the *Smash Hits Roadshow* tour, which was also to big crowds, we'd just been a support act. So now the anticipation was immense.

It was for us too. I'd been looking forward to it all my life.

I'll never forget it. I couldn't breathe for about three songs – I literally couldn't catch my breath. It was unbelievable. And the heat – it was so intense. Standing on stage in our first stage outfits for the first number was an insane feeling. I was singing the words quite well, but I was gasping, I really couldn't get my breathing right. The adrenaline was racing through me so much that I could almost feel it in my veins.

I didn't really smile that much for the first three songs because I was having to concentrate so hard just to remember the routines and breathe. Then a couple of ballads calmed things down and I managed, finally, to catch my breath. I relaxed hugely and, I'm glad to say, have stayed relaxed on stage ever since.

There's a real difference between singing in front of 3,000 people and, say, 15,000. When there are that many people there, sometimes some of them are so high up you can hardly see them. When you're singing away to the audience in front of you, you sometimes forget there's a whole other tier at the top. When there are loads of people, there are a lot more things to look at, that's for sure!

For our first two headline tours, *says Mark*, I couldn't really hear myself sing because of the screaming. We hadn't really had any coaching with regards to the mics or monitors; there was an element of being thrown in at the deep end. So for those two tours I pretty much just shouted. You get this weird feeling of trying to project your voice to the back of this huge arena – but shouting isn't going to do it!

Eventually you learn how to work the microphone and the sound system, but that takes time and we kinda learned as we went along. The expectation among some of us was that there would be dozens of people to help with vocal technique, styling, performances, studio work, all that. None of us were from stage school and maybe those sort of people have that head start on us, they've already been trained with their voice, in performance, all that. We'd only really sung at school and in musicals, and then on the Boyzone dates we'd be on stage early when the venues weren't full, and then suddenly, it seemed, we were on stage in front of 15,000 people. I'd be standing there, eyes staring, mouth as wide open as possible, thinking, *Fuck me, 15,000 people need to hear this!* I must have looked like I was on drugs!

I later developed a trick, or technique if you like, that I use to this day, particularly with TV appearances where I feel awkward. I'll see someone in the room or in the crowd and I'll go, *Right, you're the one I'm going to impress now,* and I'll pretty much sing to that person. I won't look at them all the time, and they probably won't even notice I'm doing it, but it helps me focus and perform. I might just see a fan in the crowd who looks like someone who I know, for instance, and I'll pick them.

It doesn't happen every night, by the way. Some nights I don't see a person, but then the next night I will see someone and the whole

gig will be based on what they are going to say when they get home.
Maybe it'll be someone who just looks like they are enjoying themselves or someone who's singing along, and that person will make
me go for it. It really helps.

One funny aside from that is when we first started I had a bit of
an issue with waving. Where I come from, if someone waves to you
in the street, you wave back – simple manners. So we'd be playing
to, say, 15,000 people and the first 50 rows would be waving. Especially down the very front, girls would wave every time you walked
by. So I just had to keep waving back to all of them. I thought how
I would feel if I'd waved at Prince or Mariah and they'd caught my
eye and then not flickered and not waved but moved on. So I would
wave and wave and wave and wave, all night. It was getting ridiculous – there were times when I was spending more time waving
back – so as not to be rude – than I was holding the mic!

On our very first concert tour, *laughs Kian*, once we were offstage,
we went ballistic. We felt like superstars and we drank like fucking
nut jobs. I'm not even sure I want to explain what went on! We'd
been doing two years' solid promo with no tour and virtually no days
off since it'd all started. Then, in typical Westlife fashion, the first
tour we ever did was humongous – we did nine Wembleys, thirteen
nights in Dublin, six Newcastles, six Manchesters, six nights in
Glasgow, three in Birmingham, three in Sheffield and then were
overseas for nearly three months. It was four months of the most
massive shows.

That was only the half of it, though.

Behind the scenes, there was just an explosion of pent-up energy.
Young lads, well known, in all the magazines, songs in the charts,

money coming in, out on the road together – to be totally honest, we went ga-ga!

We drank very heavily every single night. Vodka and Red Bull was our favoured tipple and we sank it by the gallon. Our security man Paul Higgins reckons Shane and myself drank ourselves into oblivion for over 50 nights straight.

We were like caged animals being let loose. The situation was so different from promo – there was no record company telling us to get to bed or behave ourselves. We never needed to get up early. You'd have all day to relax before the show the following night. All the people on the tour were being paid by us. We were the bosses, so we did what we wanted, when we wanted.

And what we wanted was to party.

Mark: Actually, we were sponsored by Red Bull, so really we were just doing the right thing by our sponsors ...

A memorable day in the history of Westlife, *says Kian*, was in Sheffield on that first tour. I'll never forget it. We had a run of three shows so it felt like a mini-residence. We found this little bar around the corner from the venue which seemed ideal for our parties after each show. One of our security team went around and spoke to the manager and enquired about letting us use the bar for our aftershows.

It was a great little pub, full of weird and wonderful characters, mostly big stocky dudes who all drove Ferraris. They made us very welcome and we partied there every single night of our Sheffield stay. On one particular night, a lot of us had brought friends over and everyone was absolutely steaming drunk. Even the truck drivers, man, they loved us because they would joke and say, 'Where's the party tonight?' and we'd say, 'Follow us!' so we'd race over to this bar followed by all these massive truck drivers ready to get wrecked.

It was pure carnage. Someone was going around on a leash; one of Nicky's best friends, Skinner, was drunkenly pretending to be a priest, taking a bucket of water around and blessing people; folks were running around absolutely slammed on the bar; music was on full blast all night; Nicky was standing on the bar with shades on pretending to be Bono – it was nuts. All our dancers, all our crew, all of us, all our friends and family went mad. The barmen were just chucking drinks at us and we were chucking them down our gob. By throwing out time, we were cuckoo.

One of the bar owners offered to give me and my brother Gavin a lift home in his Ferrari as he hadn't been drinking. It was only a two-seater, but we weren't missing out on this.

'Come on, Gav, lesh get in, it'll be fucking greeaaatt!'

Gavin sat in the passenger seat first and I basically sat on top of him, completely bladdered. Then I had one of those moments of seriousness that you only get when you're blind drunk.

'Hey, Gav, whereshfuckingsheatbelt...?' I wrapped it around him and me and said, 'At leasht if we die at 150 milesss an hour, we'll die together, eh, Gav?'

This didn't seem to comfort him too much.

The bar owner then proceeded to do about 130 mph down the motorway with me and Gavin absolutely ossified out of our faces in the passenger seat.

We made it back to the hotel and continued the drinking at full tilt. Gav was actually a secondary school teacher and by about 4 a.m., he was absolutely fucked. We bundled him off to bed – for a guy who is ten years older, he did pretty well!

We got up around one in the afternoon very much the worse for wear. I had to abandon some promo interviews because I couldn't stop giggling and I was still drunk. I knew Shane was doing some interviews in his dressing room, so I headed for there, thinking he would be organized and sober and might calm me down and get me back on track.

I walked in to find him sitting slumped in the corner on his own, wearing only his boxer shorts and a pair of white sunglasses with blacked-out lenses ... and on his head was a pair of deely-boppers with flashing stars at the end of each bouncy wire.

'Hey, Kian, what's the craic?' was all he could muster.

We were due on stage in about five hours.

He was still completely twisted from the night before, off his chops on 20 shots of vodka and Red Bull. I sat next to him, laughing out loud, and thought we could both sit there and sober up together, when Paul Higgins, our security man, raced in and said, 'Kian, Kian, you've got to come, Brian's acting all weird, you've got to sort him out ...'

To be fair, I was in no fit state to sort anyone out, but if the choice was either me or Shane, then it was gonna be me. I went out to the tour bus to find Brian also twisted on vodka and Red Bull, telling everyone that the walls were closing in on him and that there was something wrong with him.

'You fucking eejit, sit down will ya ...?'

We walked around a bit and Shane came out of his dressing room, still with his bouncy stars on, saying, 'I think I need some sleep ...'

Eventually, we all surfaced from the drunken stupor and prepared ourselves for the show that night. Shane got some sleep, we all sobered up and started to feel human again.

As I followed Shane up the steps to the stage, where 12,500 people were waiting for us, he leaned over a bucket and vomited.

'Shit, are you OK to go on, Shane?' I asked.

'Yeah, yeah, it's OK, it's all out of me now. Let's go.'

He jumped up onto the stage, said, 'Hello Sheffield!' and we all proceeded to play a blistering show.

I have to say, in my opinion, the partying *never* affected our shows. We were kids – well, 21 – and we were bullet-proof. Plus, we were from the west coast of Ireland, so we had a background of heavy drinking, you know.

The drinking carried on the next day.

And the next.

And the next, and so on for the whole tour.

And the tour after that.

Shane: I don't recall being sick right before I went on stage, but perhaps I was still in no fit state to remember. I didn't learn my lesson, either. We just went on drinking, as Kian says.

That night in Sheffield, I had trouble breathing in some of the songs and I probably should have gone to hospital and got it all pumped out of my system. I remember being in an interview with Sky News the next day and I had big dark glasses on. People probably thought I was on drugs, but I wasn't, I was still very, very drunk from the vodka and Red Bull.

Vodka and Red Bull is a mad drink. I was a nutbag on it. I'd go out with Gillian to a club and I'd be drinking it and forget about her for an hour and a half, just be chatting to people, having a laugh, and eventually Gillian would be like, 'Where were you?' So, eventually I stopped drinking it, because it just didn't agree with me.

But, come on, we were young fellas, we were 20, 21, out having a laugh and we were famous. We were in this band, it was amazing, we were selling out everywhere, we had money in our pockets, it was like pure joy.

What's the point doing all the work if you can't enjoy the benefits?

We just kinda enjoyed them a bit too much.

Nicky Kian Shane MARK xx

CHAPTER ELEVEN

SOUVENIRS FOR THE SOUL

The first time we went to South East Asia, *recalls Mark*, it was such absolute hysteria. We'd sold so many records there. *Coast to Coast* had taken over as the biggest album of all time in Indonesia. I think it toppled *The Bodyguard* by Whitney Houston. We were told at the time that the album had sold a million copies and that the black market was usually five to one, so that gives you an idea of how popular we were. As soon as we landed, there were thousands of fans at the airport and that was how it was until the minute we took off at the end of the trip.

I loved Indonesia, it was such a beautiful country and the people were so warm and welcoming. The hysteria was something else, though. Bear in mind we'd only been signed just over two years and here we were on the other side of the world, having to helicopter out from the roof of our hotel to get away safely, flying off over the heads of the 5,000 fans camped out below.

Strangely, one of the most memorable incidents there was to do with the police and security forces, rather than the fans. They were sharing the security duties between them and it was obvious to us that there was a lot of tension about who was actually in charge. At one particularly mad show, there were about 300 of each, so it was a big presence.

Normally after those shows, we'd come offstage and get changed, maybe have a quick chat then head to the hotel. But this time the tour manager came straight over to us as we walked off and said, 'Quick, quick, get in the tour bus, quick!'

We didn't know why, but jumped in anyway, leaving our crew to finish up. They said that after we'd left, the police had lined up on one side of the stadium, the security forces had lined up on the other side and basically they'd run at each other and had a massive scrap in the middle of the venue, this huge brawl. And these were the people in charge of keeping a lid on things!

We got to meet local dignitaries, princes, kings, crazy stuff, all around the Far East. Perhaps the best night like that was when the Sultan of Brunei asked us to give a private show for him. He'd built an amphitheatre for Michael Jackson to do a gig and we were the next band to play afterwards.

Hanging round with the Sultan's family was great fun. He had a personal bowling alley and fun park and we were given the keys, basically, to go on any ride we liked for as long as we liked. All his family were there and every one of them had a beautiful Porsche or Lamborghini or Ferrari, and they let us all have a race around in those. It was like a schoolkid's dream – amazing. And perhaps the best part of it was that alcohol was illegal, so we were just living off the buzz of it. I remember at the time I thought, *What other job would enable you to do this?* It was incredible.

The hysteria for Westlife in that corner of the world hasn't really died down. One time we were back in Indonesia and towards the end of the dates I decided to have a massage at a health spa. It had been a tough few weeks travelling and I felt like a treat. A woman came in and proceeded to do the massage, and it was lovely, very relaxing. Then, as I lay there completely naked, with only a small white towel around my waist, she pulled a phone camera out of her bag and said, 'Mr Mark, can I take picture please?'

One of my biggest memories from South East Asia, *recalls Kian*, was a showcase. Normally, you do these events for the media and the industry. There are perhaps about 200 or so invited guests in some pretty small room and you go in and sing a five-song set, shake some hands and generally charm the people who are considered to be important in that territory.

Well, in Indonesia, they like to do things a bit differently. We turned up for a showcase to find over 6,000 people there. It was supposedly a low-key industry function, but it was like the maddest gig you could imagine. There were girls throwing themselves at the stage, being pulled out of the front rows, fainting, the full works. I made the mistake of putting my hand near the crowd and I swear my fingers were nearly pulled out of the sockets. It was nuts. Then this one girl in the front row was dragged out and taken to one side, sat down and given some water. Suddenly, she sprang up, ran onto the stage, raced across in front of us and launched herself onto Mark. He was just standing there by his mic with this fan wrapped tightly around him – two arms, two legs, clamped on him for dear life.

Two security men came on, prized her fingers apart and pulled her off like a piece of meat. As they were dragging her off the stage, she was still screaming, 'Mark! Mark! Mark!' It was an absolute classic.

Let me tell you about scissors, paper, rock, *says Nicky*. It's a major part of the Westlife story. We make a lot of decisions using the old favourite game. Got to do a late-night international phone interview? Scissors, paper, rock. Standing in the middle of a *Smash Hits* front-cover photo? Scissors, paper, rock. Who's got to go first through a gauntlet of 3,000 grabbing hands and screaming girls ...? Yup, scissors, paper, rock.

After one of these Indonesian shows, *recalls Shane*, I remember some fans pinning Kian up against the side of the bus and one girl just ripping his chain necklace off him. It was insane. To me, it felt like the nearest we could get to what you read about Beatle-mania.

Given how important it had been for me to keep my family ties close when we signed that record deal, *explains Mark*, I was gutted beyond belief to discover that for my twenty-first birthday we would be abroad. There was no way around it – it was our first world tour, there were big shows booked and I would be thousands of miles away from home. I was devastated.

On the night of my birthday, the crew made up some excuse about having to sign visa forms in one of their rooms and when I got there, everyone had thrown a huge surprise party. I was so shocked! I'd been so fed up I just hadn't seen it coming. They'd taken over the function room on the top floor of the hotel and kitted it out with catering, food, balloons and a karaoke machine. All the musicians had brought their instruments along, because they knew I'd love a bit of a sing-song. It was the best party, I really loved it and it meant so much to me that people had made that much effort.

I woke up the next day with a massive hangover, handcuffed to the bed, but someone had lost the key and my hand was all swollen and purple! Still, it was worth it and, besides, I had an easier time of it than one of the tour manager's assistants – she was blind drunk on the floor, handcuffed to a table for about four hours screaming, 'Let me out! Let me out!', when all she needed to do was lift the leg of the table and walk off.

We knew South America could be crazy, *recalls Nicky*. One of the security lads had been told by a fortune teller there was going to be an 'incident'. I wasn't married or had kids at the time, but I took out life insurance and made a will. It shows you how volatile it can feel. Nothing happened, fortunately, although we did have to have armed convoys because we were considered a high kidnap risk – not exactly your *Smash Hits Roadshow*!

I love Brazil, *smiles Kian*. We've had some of our best times there. That time we had to do the radio interview on the roof of the coach was very typical of the hysteria that followed us around.

After that mad rooftop interview we finally got the bus out of the crowds and headed off for a TV appearance. Fans were driving alongside us on the main roads, hanging out of the windows of their cars to get pictures. We went into the studio and were walking down a corridor as we were being miked up. The record company guy said, 'It's a very popular slot. Two girls are the interviewers. You'll like it very much. It's called *Naked News*.'

I looked at Brian. Brian looked at me.

We walked around the corner and there stood two beautiful Brazilian girls, completely naked but for a thong the size of a small piece of string.

Well, it was better than being on *Jonathan Ross!*

*   *   *

Next up was America, *ponders Nicky*. We'd pretty much conquered the UK, most of Europe, to be honest most corners of the globe, and we were doing well everywhere, but we hadn't yet had a crack at the States.

We turned up in New York airport really excited. We were all so fired up about taking on the US, but straight away it was a bit like being the Leeds boot boy again – we were like, 'Yeah, we're here, we've had all these number 1s, look!' and they'd go, 'Whatever. D'you want a cab?'

The business parts of the jigsaw seemed to all be in place, *says Kian*. We were signed to RCA Records and our key man over there was the legendary Clive Davis, who had famously signed Whitney Houston, Aerosmith and Janis Joplin, among many others. He loved the two albums we gave him and wanted to follow pretty much the same plan: 'Swear It Again', 'If I Let You Go', then 'Flying without Wings'. We shot a new video for 'Swear It Again', which was a bit daft, to be honest with you. We were all at a carwash with these girls and Shane was sharing an ice cream with one of them. It was a wee bit corny, you know. But at least they were having a go with us.

They put 'Swear It Again' out and we then had about eight weeks of touring.

As we drove along these endless American highways, we started to learn how very different that market is from the UK. It was all about radio 'spins', airtime, audience share ... Radio ruled everything. The single went in modestly but started to climb and climb. It was heading in the right direction.

We were very happy to put some graft in on the road. We'd just come from Asia via South America and we were all really exhausted, but excited about being in the States, hanging out in New York, LA, all the famous places. We flew so many times, it was incredible, all these short internal flights. A typical day would involve an early-morning flight to a radio appearance, maybe with a studio performance on air, then you'd jump on another plane and do an afternoon open-air gig at, say, 3 p.m., then you'd race back to the airport and catch a 6 p.m. plane and do another gig, where you were first on the bill, at an evening show. Sometimes we'd be on the same bill as people like Bon Jovi, but literally first on, way before many people had even turned up. We were flying around all these little places in America, places I wouldn't even remember the name of – football fields, small venues, large festivals, everything. We did this sort of schedule for weeks and weeks.

One TV appearance was an absolute Westlife classic. We were booked to appear on a home-shopping channel. One of the guys in the record company had had the brainwave of putting us on there. The idea was that we'd sing a few numbers and maybe chat to the host, then they'd sell our CD.

'That was Westlife, ladies and gentleman, and if you buy their CD in the next 20 minutes, you'll get it for the special price of $7.99, and we'll even get them to sign it for you.'

To be fair, it was actually quite a cunning plan.

On paper.

The studio was in the arse-end of nowhere and it took forever to get there. We went in and did the songs, did the chat and sat back waiting for the phones to light up with excited buyers.

One of the staff kept coming up saying, 'It's going great, you guys! The phones are ringing off the hook!'

We were really pleased; we'd been a little apprehensive about this, but it seemed to be working.

'Hey, you guys, more calls! This is just great!'

Then, after about half an hour, I said to them, 'Er, excuse me, how many albums have we actually sold?'

'Like 2,000 or something. Isn't that great, you guys?!'

'Great, yeah.'

'Oh, look! More calls!'

'Excuse me, out of interest, how many copies did the number 1 album sell in America last week?'

'1.4 million.'

In among all the hard work, *recalls Nicky*, we made sure we found time to party. One night in San Diego we had to go out with a radio woman who had the reputation of being something of a real tough cookie. America was still not really loving us, so we were going all out to win people like her over. We met up with her – a real tomboy – and she suggested going to an Irish bar.

'I hear you Irish boys can drink, is that right?' she said.

'We have been known to have the odd gargle,' I replied. 'If you want to go on the piss with us, we'll have a drinking competition with you, but we're after drinking Irish shots.'

She was well up for this and called someone over. We immediately noticed the waitress's accent and it turned out she was from Sligo. This radio woman was like the queen, sitting in this bar loudly ordering a round of drinks. She ordered triple vodka shots and then asked us what we wanted.

'Can we have your very strongest, most potent *uisce*, please?' I said to the Irish waitress with a grin. 'Only the best stuff, mind.'

Uisce is Irish for 'water'.

So we proceeded to slug shot after shot of water, downing them like hard spirits, while the radio woman slammed triple vodka after triple vodka after triple vodka down her neck. She was absolutely blazing drunk, I mean *balloobered*.

'Jeshus, you Irishhh boysh can drink ...' she stammered as we sank back our last measure of water.

The next day the feedback from her office was that she'd had a brilliant time, we were lovely lads and, most of all, we could drink like fish. She *loved* us.

She still didn't add our single to radio, though!

I felt like we got our own back on the American record business in a very small-minded and childishly devious way though, later during that trip! I played a trick on a record label guy. I said, 'I'll give you 50 bucks if you can hide this coin anywhere on your body and I can't find it.' He fancied his chances, so while he hid it, I went out to the parking lot and ran all my fingers on the dirty, oily inside of a car's exhaust.

I came back and started frisking him all over his face, mouth, ears, hair, hands, and by the time I'd finished with him he was covered in soot. But of course he didn't know that and was just really pleased to win. It was priceless. Well, not exactly priceless – it cost me $50 – but it was worth it!

Another time, *laughs Kian*, we all wanted to go clubbing but we were still underage, except for Nicky. So he went to the front of the queue and spoke to the bouncer, who said, 'Let me see some ID.'

Nicky showed him his passport and the bouncer said, 'Alright, come in.'

As this guy turned to move the velvet rope, Nicky palmed his passport behind his back to me.

Nicky went through and I was now at the front of the queue.

'OK, let me see some ID.'

I showed him Nicky's passport, holding it with my hand over his photo.

'Alright, come in,' and again he turned to move the rope.

I palmed the passport back to Shane and the bouncer let me through ...

I swear all five of us got in that club on one passport.

We did a lot of roadshows in the US alongside really big acts like Britney Spears and, one time, Eminem. We saw him backstage and he pretty much sneered at us and said, 'Hey, so you're supposed to be the new Backstreet Boys, huh!' and laughed. I thought, *Yeah, you motherfucker, we fucking are, mate, so fuck off,* but I didn't say anything.

There were some encouraging signs in the States – we shifted 250,000 singles in a couple of weeks, something we'd have had to work, say Germany, for six weeks to two months to achieve. We went on to shift half a million and I have my only American disc to show for that on my wall. Part of the problem was, we were having to spread ourselves thin, because while America was pretty indifferent, the rest of the world was begging for us, everybody and their mother, literally. It was nobody's fault, it was just that so many territories were after us.

Another complication, albeit later, was that Ruben Studdard from *American Idol* released 'Flying without Wings', which we felt was our golden ticket. Once he'd put that out in the States, our momentum struggled.

Then our key man, Clive Davis, left the record label. The new guy was very enthusiastic and behind us, but we were selling eight million copies of our second album worldwide and we had to go and promote it elsewhere. There were other factors too, some political within the business, but also the climate in America was turning against pop bands.

I'm skipping ahead of myself a little here, but a good example was when we did a white label of 'World of our Own' the year after we first toured the States. We'd shot a brilliant video in a disused building in Dublin – we looked good, it was a superb clip and everyone was delighted – and then, because we'd had resistance on the past promo tour, the record label very cleverly put the song out in the clubs and to radio as a white label only, no band name, nothing about us, just the record company logo stamped on the bottom of it.

Our radio plugger called us and said the phones were lighting up, people were loving it ... but ...

'But what?'

'Well, then they insist on finding out who the mystery hit is by and when I tell them Westlife, they literally say, "Oh, a boy band. We don't play boy bands anymore, bye, bye."

It was as brutal as that.

Mark: The American music industry is a lot more cut-throat than the UK. The executives in the UK have much better people skills. In America, there's a kind of fakeness. It's so transparent but they don't care it's transparent and if you've got a problem with that then you're being unprofessional.

Also, during one particularly long trip, my grandfather died, so it was all pretty awful. As you know, he was a very special part of my childhood, so I was devastated. He had been so proud of Westlife, too. I flew back and Ronan Keating very kindly leant me his jeep to drive home. I made it to the funeral and sang a song too. I really wanted to be there to support my mum. It was a big blow. I learned so much from my grandfather, so he will always be with me.

That time in America was really tough and broke all our backs.

Two of the biggest fights in the band happened in America on that first big tour, *recounts Kian*. Brian thought about going home after about five weeks, he was pretty fed up. Then Brian and Nicky had a huge fight in a diner one day and Nicky got up and said he'd had enough. He went outside, rang Louis and said he was going home. It was all sorted out, but the tour was too long and we'd been halfway round the world first. It was just a case of being away for too long.

Living out of a suitcase isn't easy. In our first year we worked 180 days in a row, without a single day off. It was incredible – several flights a day, all over the world. It was just 'Get your suitcase, go, go, go!'

It was all so crazy, *recalls Mark*, but the word 'no' wasn't in our vocabulary when it came to putting things in our schedule. If you even suggested not doing anything, you felt that you were literally the most unprofessional and ungrateful person.

I just felt that, in general, you know. I wouldn't point the finger at the label or Louis or anyone else, it was how *I* felt. There was always this big desire to impress the record company, to make them think that you wanted this *so* much. So we didn't get a day off for those 180 days, no, but to be fair we never asked for a day off.

I think in the first few years, *continues Kian*, everybody had a moment when they were like, 'I'm going home, I'm getting on a plane and going home to my three-bedroomed semi in Sligo and I couldn't give a flying shit about all this.' But none of us went.

In those early years I had very much a one-track mind; it was all Westlife, Westlife, Westlife. If one of the lads was after going home or even just having a few days off, I was pretty hard on them. 'Come on, this is it, this band is working, we're on top of the world, why would you want to go home? How *could* you go home? You're in a massive band, selling records all over the world, we're in Mexico, are you stupid?' I chilled out an awful lot later on, but back then I was all one-track.

It was naïvety on my part. Nowadays, I'd do it differently, I'd listen more to what they were saying, I'd maybe get in touch with people and try to arrange schedules differently. To be fair to the lads, they never complained and always did the work. They were brilliant. But I was naïve.

Never, not once, did I want to leave the band, *says Shane*. There were days when I didn't want to be doing it, perhaps I was tired or I wanted to be at home or maybe I was missing my best mate's twenty-first birthday and they were all out in Sligo and I was in the Philippines. Yes, there were days when you didn't want to be there. But never once have I felt I don't want to be in the band or to be a pop star, to live the dream.

During the period when we worked those 180 days straight, *winces Nicky*, I had a hernia! I'd picked it up during my time at Leeds. It's very common for footballers, but I hadn't got it sorted. I used to stand for photo shoots with the band and it would kill me, though, so I eventually had to get it fixed. Even that was hard to organize, because our schedule was so frantic. I didn't tell the label for a while, to be honest. It seemed too inconvenient.

We all wanted to crack America, *continues Kian*, and I'm not going to lie to you – we were all very disappointed when it didn't turn out as we'd hoped. But d'you know what? Looking back with the benefit of hindsight and a good few more years under our belts, it wasn't the end of the world. What's more, I do wonder if we had exploded in America like we were exploding all over the rest of the world at the time, it would have finished us.

We never underestimated the graft you needed to do to crack the States, but if we had broken that market, I think we might have become completely arrogant arseholes – because at times it felt like everything that we tried just worked. If America had fallen too, there'd have been no way of keeping us on the ground. We'd have completely different lives. We'd have cracked every major territory in the world within two albums – and don't get me wrong, that would have been brilliant, that would have been our preference – but you have to wonder what the repercussions would have been on our personal and professional lives.

Would we have even still been together as a band ten years later, if we'd cracked America back then? I think probably not.

CHAPTER TWELVE

CELEBRITY SKIN

When we first started in Westlife, *recalls Mark*, it was like an atomic bomb going off in our lives. Suddenly we were on the telly, in the papers, all over the radio, breaking records, having hits, selling albums by the million. Inevitably, you find yourself presented with certain situations, being offered drugs or other temptations. It's the nature of the beast that is the music business.

We all come from pretty similar Irish families, a certain type of background. What was brilliant, looking back, was how our families warned us all off drugs. Everyone, just *everyone*, did. We were kids, we were famous and we were earning a lot of money at a very young age and that's a recipe for disaster. You don't need me to tell you of the high-profile casualties who've fallen into that trap. The people who cared about us didn't want to see it happen to us.

Our families warned us off drugs so much that the first time I was offered cocaine, I was absolutely terrified. Coke is the drug of the music business and you can go to certain events and it's everywhere. I ran a mile when I was first offered it; I'd built it up into such a terrifying thing.

I laugh when I look back, because I was so naïve to the wider world when we first started that I thought that people would be throwing coke at us on stage at *Top of the Pops*, that they'd virtually be stuffing it up my nose for me. I pictured photo shoots where they'd bring trays of cocaine around instead of having tea breaks.

The reality is I've been offered cocaine perhaps three times in ten years. The other boys may say different, but that's all I've experienced.

One of these occasions it was a perfect music business cliché. I was at the Met Bar a few years into Westlife and I was chatting to some people when they asked if I'd like some coke. 'Er, no, thanks,' I said quickly. I was scared of it, you know, which is a good thing because it kept me away from it. I felt like it was such a cliché.

The flipside of this was that with our image being so apparently 'clean cut', people assumed we were far more strait-laced than we actually were. Take that first debauched tour as an example! People would initially ask us about drugs, almost to see our response and maybe point the finger, but then as it became apparent that we weren't about to collapse from a crack cocaine addiction, the questions stopped. We didn't do drugs, we didn't fall out of nightclubs all the time and we didn't have punch-ups with photographers, so there wasn't much for them to cover.

I always say we're not clean living and we're not crazy bastards, we're just somewhere in the middle. We try to go to the gym, but by the end of January, we stop going as much. We try to eat health-

Playing the lead in *Godspell*, alongside my best friend, Rowen.

Saving one of three penalties out of five in a cup final for Home Farm, 1991.

stage for *Grease* at Summerhill College.

Singing on stage in Hawkswell Theatre aged 16

The original line-up of IOYOU.
Left–right: Derek, Kian, Michael, Shane, Mark and Graham.

The day we auditioned for Simon Cowell – note Shane's blonde hair.

Playing guitar on stage on our first tour.

Our second Record of the Year for 'My Love'.

Our mums and dads celebrate our first number 1, in Sligo.

At yet another random airport.

Being awarded the Freedom of Sligo with Mayor Rosaleen O'Grady – a very proud moment.

Kian and Mark hung-over in an airport in South Africa.

In Indonesia, we were each assigned two bodyguards.

With Puff Daddy.

Shane and Nicole in a recording s[...] in London (she is 6 weeks old) reco[...] the Face to Face album.

Shooting the video for 'Fooled Again' in Mexico.

'Hey, Bill, what's your favourite Westlife track?' Mixing with politics was easy for me.

Flying over the audience on our second tour.

Singing 'That's What Friends Are For' at the Arista 25th Birthday Party. Left-right: Clive Davis, Monica, Kenny G, Barry Manilow, Carole King, Natalie Cole, Dionne Warwick and Westlife.

Our mums meeting the Pope.

Kian's mum, Patricia.

Mark's mum, Marie.

Shane's mum, May.

Nicky's mum, Yvonne.

Presenting Simon Cowell with Celebrity of the Year award, 2004

At a video shoot with Miss Ross.

Us with the gaffer, Louis Walsh.

'You Raise Me Up'
... what a song.

A billboard on The Corner
Shop, where we used to hang
out as kids after school.

Our first trip to Dubai for a concert: five Rollers for five members. Getting the royal treatment. What a day!

ily on the road, but some days we just eat crap. Some nights we get absolutely bladdered, some nights we don't drink at all. Somewhere in the middle. Consequently, the media stopped following us around. It's hardly a big headline, is it: 'Bunch of Irish lads get drunk' Nothing to see, move along! That's very lucky, because we can enjoy ourselves but not get our personal lives torn apart, and for that I am very grateful.

I think that you just always have to have your guard up, though. You kind of ... not fend things off, but you have to stay strong. Sometimes it's not the fame, the money or the circumstances that cause problems, it's just the person. There are people who've been in bands from the age of 17 who are addicted to drugs. I started in a band at that age and I'm not off my tits on drugs all the time. I didn't end up turning into a lunatic, so it's probably in a person's blood from the start. Everyone is different and reacts to things in different ways.

It is a weird thing for your ego to deal with. Your day-to-day life is made up of so many jobs – singing in front of thousands of people, doing interviews, radio, TV, visiting sick kids in hospitals, travelling abroad for charities, having a private life, it's such a mix. Consequently, you might find yourself being adored by several thousand people who worship the ground you walk on one minute and talked down to like you're worthless or have no feelings the next. It's confusing and you have to work hard to stay grounded.

Trying to look at the excess and temptation objectively, being in a pop band rather than a rock band probably helps. When we started, there were only a few pop magazines, *Smash Hits*, *Top of the Pops* magazine and so on, and you were hardly going to read about the latest singing heroin addict in those pages. Plus, coming from Ireland, as I've said, we'd seen so little of the drug culture, and because we go back to Ireland so much, that extracts us from the 'scene', especially in London.

Maybe the media has changed since we started. I know if Britney had been doing drugs way back then, no one would have known about it; now it's on the front page of every celebrity magazine. Maybe I'm just reminiscing, but I do think the media have focused more and more on that aspect. Some magazines have definitely changed the tone of their coverage. I forget how many times I've seen a picture of some celebrity stumbling out of a club with white powder up their nostrils, all shot in perfect close-up by a waiting pap. Maybe the reality talent search shows have exposed more of the behind-the-scenes side of it, or maybe it's become more acceptable to dig deeper? I don't know the answer, I'm just thinking out loud. But it did seem a bit more fun and carefree when we first started, and I'm grateful for that. It seems very different now. That change is tough on new bands; it's a much harsher climate than we had.

I'm not ashamed to say that I have never taken drugs, *interjects Shane*. In fact, I'm very proud of that. It's one thing I promised my mum. When I joined the band, she said, 'Don't get involved in drugs, whatever you do. You can drink and have a laugh, whatever, but don't get messed up on drugs please.'

I've personally been offered cocaine twice. It's not something I look at as being cool. It's sad. You can get hooked up on it and then you're fucked. I've got a beautiful family, a dream job – why would I want to mess that up by taking drugs?

Westlife has this clean-cut image – the men in suits and all that – but you know now that there's a lot more to us than that. However, one thing I am happy to say we never did was play around behind people's backs on the road. Remember, Nicky and myself have been with our partners since this all kicked off. And nowadays Mark has Kevin and Kian has Jodie, and we just don't mess about.

Of course, there were temptations, especially in the earlier days. There was temptation in every field: if you wanted to do drugs, you could have very easily sought out pretty much anything; if you'd wanted to sleep with loads of girls, you could have done that very easily. They were there for you on a plate in every different shape, size, colour and nationality – you choose, like.

I was never interested. I'd been in a serious relationship for two years before the band started and, in my opinion, Gillian was the perfect woman for me. So why mess about? Some blokes always think the grass is greener, but that's a fool's game. Travelling the world and being in a high-profile pop band, of course you see beautiful women all over the place and of course you might think a certain girl is very pretty or attractive. But that's all I would think. I'd never be such an eejit as to go behind Gillian's back. I actually don't think I could do it. Nobody is worth the risk of losing what I have with Gillian, nobody.

Besides, I have the biggest conscience in the world when it comes to my wife. I just can't keep anything from her. I'll rush in from a tour and say, 'You'll never guess what so-and-so said ...' Playing the field has never interested me, and that's being straight up and honest with you. The only temptation I gave into was drink and parties, but even that was our way of letting off steam. Some bands might read that and think not shagging groupies in every country isn't very rock 'n' roll, but that's their choice. It isn't mine.

It's not just drugs that are part and parcel of the music business and celebrity, *says Mark*. There's a huge focus on appearance and image, and that has been something I've had to deal with over the years. I felt under pressure about my weight for a long time. Once somebody from the Westlife camp went into my hotel room and took all the sweets out of the mini-bar. It got quite petty.

It wasn't until about halfway through the band's first ten years that I decided I had to let all of this go. By then I was used to being seen by some people as 'product', I was used to being spoken about as fat – nasty stuff like that. I didn't like it though. But I knew that I wanted to continue with the dream, the band, and if that was to happen, I had to stop worrying about these things.

Part of the reason I tolerated it for as long as I did is that I don't like confrontation, I didn't like telling people to not do things, I didn't have the confidence in myself to say, 'Fuck you, don't talk to me like that, I'm an adult, I'm a human being.' People would say things, my face would drop, I'd go red and walk away. Don't get me wrong – in the grand scheme of life, I'm very aware that this isn't as hard as many, many things that people go through. All I'm saying is it certainly wasn't pleasant.

I got to the point where I realized that if I was going to continue to do the band, I had to accept that there were less pleasant sides to the industry, fact. Then, once I let go off all that, not only did I enjoy the band much more, I also realized that these comments, these people, these attitudes had toughened me up, which in the long run had helped me. Anyone who has worked with us from Day One will know how different I am now from back at the start. No one more than Louis will tell you that.

The temptations and the pressures on your appearance are just two aspects of being in a famous band. The 'celebrity' itself is another. One of the most exciting experiences of my life, without a doubt, was when we went to a Versace launch party. It was packed with celebrities, which was cool, but what was really great fun was being followed by the paparazzi afterwards. We were in a people carrier driving back to the hotel and there were loads of photographers chasing us. We were speeding along and they were pulling up alongside us, making us slow down, hanging out of the windows and sunroofs shouting, firing their flashes and banging on our windows. It was *so* exciting. It was almost like watching someone else, someone famous, getting photographed. It was *brilliant*, I'm not gonna pretend otherwise. We were in a famous band, partying courtesy of Tommy Hilfiger and being chased by paps afterwards – what's not to enjoy?!

Sometimes celebrities seem to want to play down the fun side of being well known, though. Worse still are celebrities who complain about press intrusion when they behave in a way that invites the media into their lives. If I was sick of paparazzi chasing me, I wouldn't put on a three-grand suit and go for dinner at the Ivy or to a film première in Leicester Square. If you don't want to be photographed, then don't go to the première, don't go to a famous restaurant where photographers are camped outside. You see people coming out of notorious clubs and restaurants, holding their hands up and looking all flustered, like 'I'm just having a quiet night out, I want to get to my car and not be noticed,' yet all the time they are striking a pose in the latest Jimmy Choo shoes and virtually vogueing to their limo.

It's ludicrous! If you want a quiet night out, go to your local club or restaurant where there won't be any paps. You might get a few people asking for an autograph or whatever, but you won't get in the papers the next day.

And that is exactly why those sort of fame-hungry celebs don't do that. Being photographed is their lifestyle. It's what they do. They want to be in the papers the next day.

But you can't have it both ways.

Britney Spears must have a bizarre life. She probably had a laugh the first few times she went out and was chased by the paparazzi, just like we did. But then, unlike us, it happened again and again and again, and maybe, before she knew it, it became part of her reality. Now she can't even go for a coffee without 25 photographers following her. That's scary. I can't imagine having that in my life.

On the odd occasion when I've been photographed looking a little the worse for wear by the papers, I've just laughed. It's like a glorified version of your mates texting you a camera-phone picture of you drunk asleep under a bar stool somewhere, only this way about four million people see the photo! You've got to laugh, really.

Apart from when you go to the park with your friends and take your shirt off, only to open up a celeb mag a few days later to see a picture of yourself leaning over for a sandwich with about 15 stomachs and four chins ...

I remember once, *says Kian*, a big producer asked us if the fame wasn't there, would we still do our job? All the lads have their own views on this, of course, but for me the answer was this: if there were one thing I could change, it would be the fame. I don't do Westlife for the fame. Now fame gets you into places and has certain benefits, of course! We've had some amazing experiences as a result of being famous – no one would deny that! However, I wanted to be in a successful band, rather than just a famous one. I wanted to be a performer and sing rather than just be famous. Fame is not the way the world should be; everybody is equal.

You might be surprised to know that until I was 23 I still lived in the box room at my mum and dad's house. Well, it wasn't exactly a box room, it was a converted garage. I had all our silver, gold and platinum discs plastered all over the walls.

Going back to live in Mum and Dad's converted garage was a great leveller. The boys went out and bought all these beautiful BMWs – they love their cars – but I gave me dad six grand and he went out and got me a lovely little Fiat Bravo – to replace my old Ford Fiesta!

I'm playing it down a bit here, because I did buy a fancy car soon after, a lovely BMW 3 series. My dad killed me. I drove up the road in it and he was standing at the front door and said, 'Why did you buy that? It's such a waste of money.' He was worried I was going to blow my earnings, he was looking out for me, because we hadn't yet had that much money come through. He was just being a good dad, just looking out for me. He'd never known what it was like to have a few quid, you see. He loves me to buy nice things now he knows I am more secure.

When we were kids, we used to go down to the beach and play. On the way there was a cul-de-sac with five big six or seven-bedroomed detached houses that everyone in the area admired. Many years later, when Westlife was massive and I had made decent money, one of them came up for sale, a seven-bedroomed house with three-quarters of an acre and mountains in the background.

It was stunning. I bought it and moved my mum and dad and the whole family into it. That was an amazing thing to be able to do.

Every time I go back to Sligo I always catch up with my best mate, Jason Gorman and his wife Ciara – all throughout the band experience, his friendship has been important to me because you need a group of people who are not involved in the Westlife world.

Sligo is an *amazing* place. When you're just a kid it's your whole world and you don't realize there is anything outside of your town. Yet travelling the world with Westlife has actually made me appreciate Sligo *more*, not less. I love it. I see it as a warm, happy place full of really good people. When I'm travelling, I'm forever showing people photographs of Sligo – the scenery, the area. I love it and going back there is always a great pleasure.

Shane: To be honest with you, in Sligo I never really got bad reactions from people. It's one of the reasons I built my house there and one of the reasons I still want to live there. We are Westlife and people are proud of us in Sligo; obviously there are jealous people too, but in general Sligo is a place that is definitely behind us and the people are proud of us. I'd like to think it's definitely helped Sligo as a town. We've been given the freedom of Sligo, the keys to the city, which was just fantastic. If you go to a pub there, everyone chats with you, it's completely natural. Perhaps because we are there a lot it makes it all seem perfectly normal. In Dublin, you might get a few more stares – 'There's yer man,' all that – but that's only because they don't see us every day.

I'm still best mates with a few lads from when I was a kid, so that not only helps me stay grounded, but it also means Sligo is still a place where – apart from close family obviously – I have proper friends. A few fellas in particular have always been amazing to me, unbelievable mates: Keith Moran, Paul Keavney, Brian 'Brig' Heraghty and Anthony 'Chicken' Gray. They've never let me down and when you have a job like mine, proper friends are very hard to find and trust. My brother-in-law Cathal is an amazing mate too. My friends are all priceless and I feel lucky to know them. It makes life in Sligo more normal and much richer ...

You need your best mates around to keep an eye on you while you are home, *says Nicky*. My lads, Colm Costello, Shaun 'Skinner' O'Grady, Paul Irwin and my bro-in-law, Mark Gallagher, keep me on my toes. Paul always winds me up saying we should wear balaclavas because we've robbed so many people's songs. How do you reply to that?

Occasionally, *continues Shane*, you do something, though, that you know will cause a stir. It's part of the fun. I remember one time the band all just really fancied going to the cinema. We do get on very well as a group of lads. Even with all the complications of being in Westlife and the arguments that can cause, we still love to go out and have a blast with each other just as mates.

We had a day off from some tour dates in Scotland and there was a shopping centre near to the venue with a cinema in it. We all really wanted to see *Mission Impossible III*, so that's what we did. Looking back, I can imagine how it would have looked, like some video shoot. These big double doors opened to a cinema full of people, and Westlife strolled in, all together, in a line. Everyone stopped and stared. People were virtually choking on their popcorn!

I agree with Mark, *says Nicky*, we've generally had a good experience of the media and being well known. It's changed over the years. In the beginning, we could do no wrong, every album we released, it was like, 'The boys have done it again!' It seemed that we were really taking the world by storm. *Smash Hits* and *Top of the Pops* magazine loved us too and at the time they had enormous circulations. We had front covers, huge features; we'd win all the awards you could think of from them. It was blanket good press.

Then a little further down the line, we started to get the odd bad review, and I have to be honest with you, we were shocked. Then certain magazines came out and the whole tone of celebrity coverage changed. Some of the editorial teams never liked Westlife, and boy, can you tell. The only time we seemed to be in some magazines was if we were being criticized. Either it was for dodging a paparazzi shot or it was just a straight slag-off.

Fortunately, *OK!* and *Hello* have always been kind to us. However, when I did my wedding pictures in *Hello* in 2003, I couldn't have imagined the trouble it would cause. The Irish press were pretty harsh with me for selling my wedding pictures to an English magazine, what with my father-in-law Bertie Ahern being the Taoiseach, the Prime Minister. Worse still to them, the wedding wasn't in Ireland.

I'd never even thought of it like that. It was a very lucrative offer and what that meant to me and Georgina was that we could afford to throw the most fairytale wedding for all our family and friends. We hired the Château d'Esclimont, just an hour away from Paris, had a free bar the whole weekend and invited 400 guests, no expense spared, and that could not have happened without the input of the magazine. On the day, we had our own private photographer,

John Ryan, and a DVD made of the entire event. It was all beautiful. As a couple, we had an amazing wedding day and we were giving ourselves and our families a day to remember, so it felt like a happy medium.

But the Irish press caned Georgina's dad. They caned us as a couple too. They turned on me and all of a sudden the reports about the wedding were very harsh. Our PR lady, Joanne Byrne, had a very demanding job and was getting it from all angles, from everyone. She did a great job. The media said the security was a shambles, people were booing outside – this was all bullshit. But worst of all, as Georgina drove through to the wedding in a blacked-out car, one of the press shouted at her and called her a whore.

That's not right, never will be, regardless of circumstances.

I have a few regrets – maybe we could have been a little more open with the rest of the media than we were; maybe we could have explained the exclusive deal and said, 'Sorry you can't be there on the day, is there some other way we can help out?' We had an exclusive deal for the reasons I've explained and we were always going to honour that, though. And, to be fair, I don't think we deserved the battering we got and, for a while, it killed me. I remember at the end of the year, one magazine ran a feature called 'Heroes and Zeroes of the Year' and I was the 'Zero' for marrying the Prime Minister's daughter outside Ireland.

What annoyed me the most was that the showbiz editors who slaughtered me actually knew me; they'd interviewed me for years and, I thought, were friendly. But I was only 24, so I had a lot to learn and I took certain lessons away from the wedding in that respect.

I didn't speak to some of these people for a year or so, I was so pissed off. But then I watched how Georgina's dad dealt with journalists who wrote bad things about him, terrible things sometimes, almost every day, but he kept his dignity amazingly well through it all. Eventually he stepped down in May 2008 after 11 great years as Taoiseach. I was sad for him, but on a personal level pleased for him that he would now be able to enjoy his family more and come on those holidays with his grandkids and kids that he'd had to miss over the years in office. Also, he has achieved so much for Ireland – peace in the North, a booming economy, etc., etc. Ireland is a far better place now than when he took office and I think he will be sorely missed.

Likewise, Louis was saying, 'Move on, forget it, get on with it,' and he was right. Eventually, I did move on from what was a very difficult period for me and Georgina. I tried to see it from the journalists' point of view and spoke to a few of them. They said they'd been under pressure from their editors and our wedding had been a big story to cover. I've even had drunken conversations in Dublin nightclubs where I've said, 'You bastard, how could you write that?' and, to be fair, many of them have apologized: 'I shouldn't have written that, Nicky, but the pressure was on, we needed a story.' So we've all moved on. That's the way it has to be.

I've done lots of interviews with these people since and it has all blown over now, I've been 'forgiven', it seems, but it was a shock to the system and it was the only time I'd ever been singled out like that by the media. It isn't pretty.

Mind you, you have to laugh, because sometimes you find yourself wishing they'd be more interested, not less! One time we were in India for an awards ceremony and had been asked to wear Indian gowns for the red carpet. We thought it was a great idea. We could see these shots with us wearing all the traditional gear being flashed all over the world. So we organized the costumes, complete with shoes that curled up at the end, and headed to the event. You can imagine us sitting in the car dressed like that, going, 'Don't laugh, this will be cool, this will be cool.' Anyway, when we got to the awards, there was no red carpet; in fact there was no carpet at all. There was just one guy standing there with a small camera. We were determined to get the picture regardless, so we got out of the car, walked over to him all smiles and he just went 'click' once, nodded and walked off.

Celebrity is also strange, *says Mark,* because if you're well known, you meet other celebrities and that can be even stranger than speaking to fans. And there's this weird pecking order in the magazines. It's funny when you read about A-, C- and Z-list celebrities. It makes me laugh. Who decides what you are? Beckham's an A-lister, I guess, by most standards. I often wonder what we are. I don't care, but it makes me giggle to think about it. Sometimes we are A-list, perhaps at music awards, things like that; other times, we are definitely C-list, or worse! I think we flit between levels, which is a lot of fun.

Celebrity is a very funny thing, though, even when you're involved in those circles yourself. As you know, I usually don't feel self-conscious when I sing in front of almost anyone, but there was one time when I was struggling to sing properly because of who was there.

It sounds weird because I have sung with Mariah Carey and in front of the Pope (Shane will tell you about that in a minute), Stevie Wonder, the music-biz legend Clive Davis, all sorts of famous people, singers, 'faces'. Yet the one time I really found it weird was in front of a band you wouldn't expect: the Arctic Monkeys.

I'm jumping ahead of the story a little bit here, but it shows you how weird 'celebrity' can be. We were performing at the *South Bank Show* Awards in 2007, and it was crammed with A-list names. We walked on stage and I noticed the Arctic Monkeys were sitting at the table right in front of me. I happen to be a big fan of theirs anyway, so ordinarily that would have been exciting, but as I was performing – and doing a very difficult song vocally – it was really weird.

The Arctic Monkeys are very cool. They have immense credibility. They're an amazing band. We've never had the kind of critical acclaim that they enjoy. They can't put a foot wrong, no one would argue with that. I was standing up there thinking, *They're cool, they're young, I love that band* ...

We started singing and my voice, literally, just went, *'OK, Mark, I'm going to totally fuck you over right now!'*

They were sitting ten feet away from me and I was really, genuinely struggling to sing. Now Shane, he will sing in front of *anyone*, he just doesn't worry, he's got supreme confidence. In fact, if he were standing in front of a band and thought they were sneering at him, he'd sing even better than ever just to piss them off. I'm not like that. I wish I was, but my confidence is more fragile. And that situation was made worse by the fact that it was a room full of people who weren't Westlife fans. They hadn't chosen to be there to see us.

My confidence has improved hugely over the years and it's rare for me to struggle with it now, but that night at the *South Bank Show* Awards was a funny example. More oddly, an actor called Gerard Kearns, who plays Ian from *Shameless*, was there and, that bothered me a little too. Robert de Niro could have been in the audience and

I wouldn't have batted an eyelid, but the Arctic Monkeys and Gerard completely unnerved me.

I've thought about why it bothered me so much and it's because I just wanted to know, in myself, that I was good in front of people who were good too, you know what I mean? Things like that make my day. I would have been delighted to have gone up there and done my best and it killed me that I'd done far from my best. The weird thing is I can do a really good vocal in front of ten million people on TV and I'm like, 'OK, cool, no problem,' but that night I was more nervous in front of the Arctic Monkeys and the guy from *Shameless* because they're people who I admire.

I don't actually watch loads of soaps, but another time I felt awkward was when we did a charity rounders match in Hyde Park. I ran to one of the bases and when I looked up, there was Tug from *Home and Away*. For some reason, I just wanted the ground to swallow me up. See what I mean? Celebrity is brilliant but weird!

I know when I was really star-struck, *remembers Kian*. Let me tell you about the time we were backstage at the Irish Music Awards. It's basically the Irish version of the Brit Awards. We were hanging out at the bar behind the scenes at the Point in Dublin. I was sitting there with three of my mates from Sligo, having a beer and just taking it all in, when Bono walked in.

'Hey, lads, that's yer man, Bono.'

He started walking over to where I was sitting.

Shit!

He got closer and as he walked right past me, he said, 'Hey, Kian, well done tonight, my brother.'

I was gobsmacked. Trying to be cool, I said, 'Alright, er, Bono. Cheers. Thanks very much, man.'

Getting carried away with the moment, I then said, 'Hey, Bono, these are my mates from Sligo,' and all me mates said, 'Alright, Bono, how's it going?'

'Alright, lads, how's it going?'

He walked off and we sat there for a moment in silence.

'That's yer man, Bono, virtually me mate he is,' I said, pint in hand, feeling like the king of the world. All my mates did the same, sitting there, swigging their drinks, saying, 'Yup, that's Bono.'

Then we saw the Edge coming our way.

Shit!

'Hey, Kian, nice one tonight, my man.'

I was so blown away they even knew my name. I wasn't 'yer man from Westlife', I was Kian from Westlife. I couldn't believe it.

Then Larry Mullen Junior came over and approached Nicky, asking if he could say hello to a friend of his and called Nicky by his first name too.

Madness, absolute madness.

Not everyone's so good with names as Bono, *points out Nicky*. I was on holiday in Cyprus and these two kids came up to me, all shy like, and asked for my autograph. I was happy to oblige and they ran off back to their mom, *really* excited. It was nice – how can you not enjoy seeing that?

Later that day, their mother came up to me and Georgina at dinner and said, 'Thank you so much for taking the time to sign an autograph. They thought you were David Beckham.'

PROFESSIONALLY,
WE HAVE ACHIEVED
SOMETHING VERY
SPECIAL BY REACHING
A DECADE.

Nicky

CHAPTER THIRTEEN

SUPERCAR, SUPER CAREFUL

Me and Shane are car mad, *admits Nicky*. We buy *Top Marques* magazine every week and look at all the supercars in there. When the money from Westlife started to come through, it was almost impossible not to start thinking about buying new cars. At first we had nice BMWs, that sort of thing, but inevitably we eventually turned our attention to Ferraris.

In 2002, after our second tour, I decided to take the plunge and bought a beautiful Ferrari 355 F1. Shane had a gleaming black 550 and Brian – typical Brian! – came back with a bright canary yellow one! We'd spent over £300,000 between the three of us, cash.

I'd been looking at getting a black Ferrari 360 at the same time as the lads too, *says Kian*. I phoned my mum to see if it fitted in the garage, but it didn't! It seemed like a good excuse, though – if you remember my dad's reaction when I bought the BMW, imagine if I'd driven home in a Ferrari!

We all knew it made no financial sense whatsoever to buy a Ferrari, *continues Nicky*. We knew it was flash, but we just wanted to have that ultimate lad's self-indulgence. We'd worked hard and earned the money, so it was great fun to just do it and not worry. It is a fond memory driving the 355 back to my mam's house and parking it next to my jeep and BMW – you can say materialistic things aren't important and my God, in the grand scheme, they aren't (and I speak as a father), but as an ambitious and driven man in his early twenties, I was very proud.

A few months later, we were playing in Belfast and all three of us drove our Ferraris up to the gig. We were doing about ten gigs in a row there and each night we'd park these three supercars next to each other. It looked the business. Then, one night, we all climbed in our cars and raced off together. I'm sure it must have looked like flash pop stars being flash – and it was! – but it was thrilling and satisfying and something to be proud of at the same time.

As a band, it might surprise some people to know we don't miss a trick; we are in on business meetings in minute detail. We enjoy that and see it as part of our job to stay involved at that level. Obviously, the size of Westlife's success means we can't count every bean or do tour budgets, things like that, but we know what is happening within what is effectively a small corporation. Nothing goes by without the four of us seeing it, and it's very much of a democracy, even if that can sometimes lead to conflict. Louis has always involved us and the way we've been rewarded is fantastic; we're very lucky. We work incredibly hard for those rewards, but we're very lucky too.

There is an important point to make here. It is a private matter, essentially, but this cliché of boy band members earning no money isn't the case with Westlife, let me tell you that. Without going into detail, we've all made a very handsome living from Westlife. We've been able to buy Ferraris, BMWs, houses for our families, build our own houses, enjoy all the trappings of success. One proud moment for me was being able to surprise my mam and dad with a brand new Mercedes for Christmas in 2003 – their faces were priceless – and my brother Adam with a brand new Seat Ibiza for his seventeenth birthday in 2007. Being able to do those things makes all the hard work completely worthwhile.

I just wanted a fast car, maybe two cars, that's all I wanted, *says Shane*. Cars have probably been my main downfall. Fast, flashy cars lose money. I didn't care, still don't really. I always wanted a Ferrari. The Ferrari 550 I had for a couple of years. I bought it with cash, but it cost me 13,000 euros to insure. I didn't give a fuck. I literally didn't care! I'll never forget how proud I felt when I sat in it. Suede dash – ah, it was just beautiful, black with cream leather, a beautiful car.

Something people should know about Louis Walsh, *explains Kian*, is that he really knows how to keep us grounded and together. Over the years, he's put in the odd little reality check when all around us is apparently anything but 'normal'.

One time, *recalls Nicky*, he was absolutely raging at us about an incident at a hotel. From Day One, Louis has always said, 'If there are fans outside a hotel, stop and chat with them. Give them autographs, let them take some pictures, always.' He has always been really adamant that it is the right thing to do. We agreed – but when you're just off a very long flight or you haven't slept properly for weeks, it can be hard to roll up to a hotel in desperate need of kip and have to spend an hour chatting with fans, however nice they are. However, it was the right thing to do and we always did it, no matter how tired we were.

Then one day we didn't.

We were staying at a hotel in Kilburn and there were about 40 fans outside. It was about 9 o'clock at night and we drove up in a people carrier. There was a ramp to an underground car park but this particular time we just waved at the fans, we didn't stop and get out to chat. We weren't rude or anything like that, we just didn't stop to talk.

The next day, one of these fans bumped into Ronan Keating at the airport and told him what had happened. Ronan told Louis and Louis went *nuts*. He can take your hair off when he's angry. There are certain things that he classes as absolute essentials and behaving correctly towards fans is one of them.

It's gone much further than that, *reveals Kian*. He's quit as our manager on more than one occasion. Let me give you an example. We were doing some recordings in Sweden after we'd had loads of number 1s, played to thousands of people, been all over the TV, got some money behind us, all that stuff.

We were all supposed to meet in the hotel lobby at a certain time, but we didn't all get there at once. When the last band member had finally turned up, about half an hour late, Louis turned round to us and said, 'I don't want to manage you anymore.'

We were shell-shocked. It seemed like it had come out of nowhere. Everything was going brilliantly. We didn't have a clue what he was on about.

'Why, Louis?' I asked. 'What's brought this on?'

'Well, you were like a bunch of spoilt kids on the plane over this morning, you've all arrived down here in dribs and drabs, you don't realize what you have. Your attitude stinks.'

We managed to speak to him and apologize and, although he obviously carried on as our manager, it was a real scare.

Fast-forward a few years and we'd just come off an international promo jaunt when Louis called us to a meeting. He hadn't sounded best pleased on the phone and we didn't know why, because the promo trip had gone well – there'd only really been one incident when we'd had a 'discussion' with one of the international record company fellas. We'd been on a coach in some far-flung country and had been coming out of a hotel surrounded by loads of fans. We'd had a drill for this where we took it in turns: first you'd take off anything that could be grabbed, so that might be ear-rings (they'd be ripped out), hats (gone in seconds), hair not tied up (it would be pulled out) or bags (taken or emptied). The security man would grab one of us, run the gauntlet through this sea of grabbing hands, and you'd get to the bus, sit on your chair, half-laughing, half-out of breath. It was mad. We always enjoyed it. You do hear some singers complain about it and it can be frightening if it gets too much, but it's normally a bit of craic.

Anyway, I went first, then Mark, and it was nuts, there were hundreds of pairs of grabbing hands. Shane made it through, then Nicky, but when Brian came to do it, he hadn't held his bag tightly enough and someone had managed to grab the half-open zip and rip a brand new pair of trainers out of it.

Brian was fed up, understandably. They were brand new trainers, he'd just bought them and now they were long gone. He said,

'Perhaps if I lean out of the window and explain they might give them back? Anyone fancy having a go ...?'

I chose not to suggest scissors, paper, rock ... *says Nicky.*

He knew they were probably lost, *continues Kian*, but he was just fed up and thinking about what to do.

Suddenly your record company fella erupted. 'Forget about your fucking trainers! Forget about them! They've fucking gone! We're late for a fucking TV show, so I'm not hanging about for a pair of fucking trainers!'

Shane was sitting nearby and he said, 'Alright, mate, there's no need for that,' but before he could continue, your record company fella turned on him and shouted, 'What the fuck do you care? You're going to be a fucking millionaire and what am I going to be? Fucking nothing!' Then he stormed past us to the back and punched the side of the bus.

So, to be fair, we didn't have the best relationship with this chap. Then, at the end of the trip, when we'd worked really hard for six weeks, we fancied a few beers on our last night before we flew home. This fella wasn't having it. He got us into his office and talked for around an hour about his father studying for a degree while holding a job down, all this kind of stuff. We were sitting there thinking, *Christ, we only wanted to go for a few beers ...*

In the end, he basically said that if we went out that night, he wouldn't work for us 'in the same way' – in other words, he wouldn't really bother. We were pretty pissed off, but didn't want another episode like the one on the bus, so we just went along with it, thought nothing more of it, then flew home.

Anyway, it turned out this fella had sent an email to Louis complaining about us, saying how out of control we were. I don't think we were 'out of control' – there was probably a bit of truth to it, you know, but we weren't that bad.

Louis quit as our manager again.

This was around the time of *Coast to Coast*. We were in the process of selling eight million albums and on the way to being one of the biggest pop bands on the planet. But he quit right there.

Again, we spoke with him and explained our side and it was all sorted. But it was another shock, another reality check. He keeps you on your toes, does that Louis Walsh. Fantastic.

Did I personally lose the plot? Yeah, probably. Well, maybe not 'the plot', but I look back at some of the TV interviews and stuff like that and I sound like a cocky little shit! I was the point of contact with Louis and that developed into the point of contact with the record label, the marketing manager, the TV person, the press person ... So Louis would often say, 'Speak to Kian, you'll get your answer from Kian.' I loved it; I thought it was great. It was such a big role and such a big part for the band and – trying to be brutally honest with you here – as the years went on, I thought, *I'm great.*

In some interviews, I look at myself and read what I said and you can tell that I was getting cocky. In a way, it was quite hard to avoid. I'm speaking for myself here, but I was young, I'd wanted to be in a boy band, and now we were the biggest boy band of the lot. When I was only 18 we released our first record and had seven number 1s in a row. Around this time, we sold 1.2 million copies of the Comic Relief cover 'Uptown Girl' with a video featuring the supermodel Claudia Schiffer. The world seemed to have fallen at our feet. I think it was impossible to not have an ego. It was human nature.

We don't take it for granted, *says Shane*. OK, perhaps in the early days we might have done a bit, to be fair. Every now and then, one of us would get to thinking they were great, but normally straight away the others would be like, 'Listen, you're a bit of a fucking bollocks, the way you're going on, you need to cop on like, we're not happy.' It happened to every one of us and we were all snapped straight out of it. You can't be in a band with four people who think you're a prick.

But you live and learn, *continues Kian*. You grow a little older and see that what you were saying was cocky. Thankfully, a few people around me said, 'Do you not think that sounded cocky?' Louis was even more direct – he just quit.

Nowadays, I don't think there's any need to give us a reality check because we are all a lot more seasoned and that bit older. We know the ropes and things run pretty smoothly most of the time.

Louis Walsh will cut you like a knife with his honesty. He'll turn around to you and say, 'That's stupid, what are you talking about?' but it's not personal, he just thinks what you said was stupid. In the early days, I know he was pretty blunt about our appearance, and sometimes perhaps Mark found that quite harsh, but he knows how he works now and understands Louis just wants everything to be done properly and professionally ...

It's just not in my nature to speak to anyone in a derogatory way, *says Mark*. 'If it's constructive it's fine, but if it's a throwaway comment, that's not so good ...

We know he is the man who gets the record business excited about Westlife, *continues Kian*, Take him out of the equation and you'd have a very different ball game. When the Spice Girls took Simon Fuller out of the picture, in my opinion, they weren't the same again. We were never going to make that mistake.

MARK xx   Jim   Shane   Nicky

CHAPTER FOURTEEN

THE WIDER WORLD

On our third album, *World of our Own, recalls Shane*, we started getting involved in the writing process. There were three songs co-written by me and Brian, two co-written by Nicky and Kian, and one co-written by Nicky, Kian and Mark. There were almost two camps for a while, but Simon kept everyone happy and made sure there was a good balance of everyone's work on the final album, including the band and all these famous songwriters.

The singles from that period were mostly massive. 'Queen of my Heart' sold half a million copies worldwide and 'World of our Own' shifted a further 450,000.

We actually recorded the album in Dublin, *recalls Shane*. The night before we were going to record the song 'World of our Own', we were out on the town with the producers at Lillie's Bordello. We were drinking vodka and Red Bull and got *sideways*. One of our producers got lost in Dublin, we were all bladdered and didn't finish until about 5 a.m. We went to the studio the next day around 2 p.m., and I was absolutely dying with a hangover.

'Let's have a go at "World of our Own", Shane,' said Steve Mac.

'Ah, I can hardly talk, Steve. I'm dying here ...'

Ever the professional, Steve insisted, so I went into the vocal booth still half-steaming. The song needed a lot of grit and because I was in a state, I managed to do a great vocal on it. One of the verses was done in one take. Steve loved it so much because it had so much energy on it, but the reality for me was I was half-steamed singing it.

'World of our Own' was a key song, a key moment for the band. That song is our party piece. People love it. It's one of those songs you can play five years down the line, ten years down the line, and people will still love it. It's a great song to perform, too.

The album was cool, too. It was a very good original record and without a doubt it definitely took us up a gear. At that stage, we just needed a bit of edge and I think 'World of our Own' gave us that.

That album was interesting, *suggests Kian*, because of all the behind-the-scenes writing ideas. It's not widely known that members of Westlife wrote some of the material. Part of the problem there is that in the credits, if it says 'co-write' with a songwriter, people assume that the singers didn't *really* write anything, they maybe just happened to be standing in the studio when something was composed. That's untrue, and in the case of Brian and Shane, I think they are very talented songwriters.

During that early period, we developed two distinct 'Westlife sounds', which to a lesser degree are still quite appropriate to this day. We had the Steve Mac/Wayne Hector sound from the Rockstone studio – songs like 'Swear It Again', 'Flying without Wings', 'What Makes a Man', 'World of our Own' – and then we had the Swedish sound from the team in Stockholm – very poppy, simple lyrics, strong melodies, songs like 'If I Let You Go' and 'My Love'.

Single number four was 'Bop Bop Baby', written by me and Brian. It's a great melody and had a funny video with Vinnie Jones in it, but it only went in at number 5. It sold a lot of copies, but we were all disappointed, and it didn't help that we had written it ourselves.

We'd done well with the band by that stage, *explains Shane*, and we thought maybe we could write songs. If I'm being honest, we started to think we could have a go at *anything*. Maybe we even thought we were better than we were, truthfully. We wrote some alright songs, but looking back at it now, were they good enough? They were OK, but they weren't number 1 songs.

It was an experience to see what that process was like.

Was it wrong to do it?

No.

Would we do it again?

No.

I don't think I'm a talented songwriter. I think Mark is, he has a gift for it, maybe not in Westlife's style, but he is definitely a songwriter ...

I've learned how to separate my love for songwriting from being in Westlife, *explains Mark*. I write songs for myself, for my personal enjoyment, and I just don't seem to write Westlife songs ...

I know in my heart and my soul, *continues Shane*, that I could write a song with a good songwriter, but I'm not really interested, to be perfectly honest. I just want to sing great songs. I'd rather sing a brilliant Steve Mac song than sing a quite good song of my own any day.

*   *   *

Christmas 2001 will always be remembered by the band for something other than how well our album was doing, however, *says Shane*. Without a doubt, one of the top five highlights of me life was meeting the Pope, which we did in December that year.

I was used to getting these phone calls in Westlife – me mum phoning up about Louis, Louis phoning up about supporting Backstreet Boys, all that – but when the phone rang and we were told the band had been invited to sing in front of the *Pope*, it was a *huge* deal for me. For all of us.

Each Christmas the Vatican holds a festive performance for the Pope and they invite various musicians and singers. It's a very prestigious invite to receive and we were all very proud when we got the call. Now it was my turn to surprise my mum – she is very religious and goes to Mass every few days. The Pope had come to Ireland on a pilgrimage when I was just three months old. He had gone to Knock, which is a famous place near Sligo, and a *million* people went to see him. Imagine that – 500,000 one side, 500,000 the other side, just to see one man. My mum had been one of them. Mark's mum had gone too. So had Kian's mum, who was pregnant with him at the time.

Then, 22 years later, here I was going to meet him in person and able to take my mum with me.

'Mum, er, would you like to meet the Pope?

'What?!'

You can imagine her reaction ...

The day came to go to the Vatican and we flew over to Rome in a really classy private jet. We landed in the late afternoon and checked into our hotels, but it wasn't until about 8 p.m. that some-one noticed our suits weren't there. For some reason, they just had-n't arrived with us. Our tour manager made a phone call to the Vatican and explained that we did have some smart-casual stuff we could wear, but it was an absolute no-no, it was the Pope, you had to wear a suit.

Faced with meeting the Pope the next day and not having suits, we did the only thing that seemed 'sensible' at the time: we flew our suits over from the UK by private jet. No one and nothing else on board, just the pilot and five suits.

They were expensive suits as it was, but by the time they had been flown by private charter to Rome, they must have been the most expensive suits in the world! We laugh about it now, and none of us can actually remember why on Earth we didn't have the suits with us, but in the last-minute panic, it seemed like the right thing to do.

Of course, when they got there, the suits were a little creased. Kian wanted to hang them up over the bath and run a hot shower for hours to steam the creases out, but I had visions of us standing in front of the Pope in these soaking wet, crumpled suits, so we just crossed our fingers and, luckily, the next day they looked great.

At the rehearsal, things didn't get any easier, though. There was a 100-piece orchestra in this 5,000-seat grand hall and they'd been given scores for everyone's music. We were set to play 'Queen of my Heart', which was our big single at the time, and 'Little Drummer Boy', as requested by the Vatican. We rehearsed the single and it was great, no problems. Then the orchestra started playing 'Little Drummer Boy' and immediately I knew we were in trouble. It was about three keys higher than anything we could sing. Now Mark has got a set of lungs on him and can reach some very high notes, but even he was struggling.

'Can you do this, Mark?' I asked him.

'Not a hope, Shane. I'm going to sound like Pee Wee fucking Herman.'

We mentioned this to the conductor, but he said there was absolutely no way we could change what the orchestra played, it was a 100-piece set up, they all had their music and it was simply too late to rescore the piece.

We were stuffed.

We could hardly say no to performing – it was for the Pope.

'Er, excuse me, God's Envoy on Earth, we've decided not to perform "Little Drummer Boy" because Mark says he will sound like Pee Wee fucking Herman.'

We were just standing there, trying to sing these ridiculously high notes, in despair really. Then Nicky noticed Dolores O'Riordan, the lead singer of the Cranberries, to the side of the stage, waiting to come on and rehearse her songs. Chancing his arm, he walked over to her and said, 'Listen, Dolores, you don't fancy a duet with us by any chance, do you?'

'Yeah, sure! It'll be a laugh. What you singing?'

'"Little Drummer Boy." Please tell me you know it ...' said Nick.

'For sure, no problem. I know the song well.'

The sigh of relief from us must have been as loud as the bloody orchestra.

We rehearsed with her there and then and she was fantastic. We chatted after, too, and she was an absolute sweetheart. On the day of the performance, it all went brilliantly and you'd never have guessed we'd had problems. We were saved by the skin of our teeth. Dolores saved our arses big time.

At the show, you couldn't get too close to the Pope really, he was up in his box, but afterwards, about 60 people or so were invited to meet him face to face. We were all chaperoned into this quite small room full of pews and with beautiful artwork by Da Vinci all over the ceilings and walls. It was in the Pope's house. We took our seats in total silence. We'd been given 12 invites, so the band all asked our mums and then we'd had two invites left, so we'd given one to our security's mother and one to our tour manager's mother and flown them in from Dublin. The dads had had to be left out, but they were just really pleased for their wives.

I'll never forget standing there in that room, waiting for the Pope to come in. I have never been so nervous. Not when we were auditioning for record labels, playing at Wembley, going on TV in front of millions – nothing touched it. You could put me in any Westlife moment and put it in the back pocket, for me, by comparison. I was absolutely shitting myself. I'd started sweating almost as soon as I got in there, standing upright with my hands clasped together in front of me, like at home in church, the sweat was pouring down my sides, underneath my shirt, down my back, over my forehead, my hands were soaking, it was even going down the crack of me arse. It was like a tap dripping, and all I could think was, *Please stop sweating, you're going to meet the Pope any second ...*

It was just so surreal. *The Pope, like.*

You get to meet all sorts of famous people when you're in Westlife, but there's nobody more famous than the Pope, in my opinion. Pope John Paul II was a very famous Pope, too, if you get my drift. Everyone in the world knew what he looked like.

The door clicked open and all our eyes darted across to see the Pope was entering. He was escorted in by quite a few cardinals and we could see immediately that he was very bent over. He looked really old, his arthritic fingers were clutching a walking stick and he seemed to be in some pain. He walked very, very slowly, shuffling really.

That's the Pope, like. The Pope!

I just kept saying it to myself, over and over. My eyes literally could not believe what they were seeing.

He sat down on a very ornate chair and started waving.

That's the Pope, like. The Pope!

My mum was in the row behind the band and I could see her touching her rosary beads, she was so excited. Meanwhile, I'm there, shitting myself. The sweat was going right down the crack of me arse, it was going down me legs ... I was all over the place, shaking like a leaf – completely, massively star-struck.

Then I started to think, *What do you actually say to the Pope?*

Hello, Pope.

Nice to meet you, Pope.

Hello, the Pope, nice to meet you, nice ceiling.

When it came to my turn, he put his hand out and I took it and said, 'It's an honour to meet you.' There's a picture of me at the moment he touched my hand and I actually look unhappy. I wasn't, I was ecstatic, but I was so nervous and anxious about saying the right thing that I ended up pulling this real grimace. I look like I've seen a ghost.

He spoke in Latin, something I later found out was 'Bless you, my child.'

I kissed the ring on his hand and he moved on.

Even as he moved slowly away, I still couldn't believe it had happened.

That's the Pope, the Pope!

When he came to meet my mum, I felt like the proudest son alive. You get in a big band like Westlife and you start to make a lot of money. You can buy your mum nice clothes, then nice meals, then a beautiful car and even a lovely big house. But watching her meet the Pope and seeing her face, her excitement, I realized that there was nothing I could ever do for her that would compare to that moment. She was a picture of pure happiness, disbelief, excitement, joy. She was so taken aback, one of the best days of her life, she couldn't believe she was kissing the Pope's hand. It was the best thing ever I've done for my mother, without a doubt, and a very rewarding experience as a son. To her, she's met the most famous person on Earth.

Mark: Meeting the Pope was a huge thing for me. I'm not ultra religious, but that whole experience was just so spiritual. It was like meeting Jesus' right-hand man. I know all the boys felt the same.

Coming from a Catholic family, *says Kian*, it was a big deal meeting the Pope – *huge*. It was an absolutely overwhelming experience. My mum put a black veil over her head, a sign of respect within the

Church, and I remember seeing her like that. It was amazing. I felt so, so proud to be able to do that for my mum. Incredible.

For me, *says Nicky*, meeting the Pope was one of the biggest moments ever. Coming from a Catholic family and a very Catholic country, when I was growing up everyone went to Mass. So to meet the Pope was incredible. It came at a time when everything in Westlife was happening very fast. We'd had the hits, the videos, we'd sung with Mariah Carey, all that had been so quick. But then this came along and it was incredible. Standing in that room waiting for the Pope was the only moment in my life when I was completely and utterly shell-shocked, nervous, call it what you will. It was surreal, incredible, amazing. And I know that for me and for all the lads, the very best part was making it possible for all our mums to meet him. It was a very special day.

Shane: I suppose when you meet anybody that is fairly famous, you get a nice feeling, but if you are fortunate enough to meet more and more stars, you do get more used to it. It's still a cool part of the job, but nothing compared to meeting the Pope. *The Pope!*

People often ask me which star has made me most nervous, apart from the Pope. Was it Whitney, Mariah, Stevie Wonder? And the honest answer is ... Tiger Woods.

About 2003 I started getting into golf. Brian started me off on it and after about half an hour of my first round, I was hooked. My good friend Anthony Gray – aka Chicken – is the professional at Strandhill Golf Club (www.anthonygray.com!) and he's been coaching me. It's great. I love it and even take my clubs with me on tour, so I can grab a round should there be a golf course near to whichever venue we are playing. In 2006, I went to the K Club to watch the Ryder Cup and that was where I saw Tiger Woods.

I didn't meet him, he just walked past.

I was frozen to the spot, completely star-struck.

That's yer man, Tiger Woods.

I'd seen him on the telly and I'd thought he'd made golf look so cool. I'd started playing after that and, to me personally, he is one of my undoubted idols, and one of my role models in life too. The way he's dealt with fame, the way he treats his family, the attitude he has to the ludicrous amounts of money he earns, his fighting spirit – everything about him is inspirational.

Perhaps it's because he means so much to me, he *represents* so much to me, that when I saw him walk past in the flesh, it was almost too much to comprehend.

Tiger Woods – kind of the Pope of golf, like.

Nicky Kian Shane MARK xx

CHAPTER FIFTEEN

STRANGE WORLD

By this stage, *explains Shane*, our band had established a pretty rigid set of working routines. The performance in front of the Pope came at the end of 2001 and another album was already scheduled for the following winter, this time a *Greatest Hits* record. We have always been very prolific.

Because we were releasing an album a year, there were certain times of the year when you knew you would be away from home, in a studio or out promoting. Let me explain what is a typical Westlife year.

Essentially, there are three types of 'Westlife days'. The first is the promotion day, which runs typically from September through to Christmas. This is the time we are actually promoting our most recent album. On those days a car will pick you up at half-seven or eight, you'll be driven to work at the studios, radio or TV shows and other places you are scheduled in for, and you will do interview after interview ...

Nicky: Scissors, paper, rock ...

Thanks, Nicky ... with some performances as well, until about six or seven at night. It can feel like Groundhog Day at times, and it's gruelling, but that's the nature of promotion.

Back in the day, we'd all then be dropped off at a hotel, but with our changing personal circumstances we try to get back to our families as often as possible. That isn't very often sometimes – in the last ten years, we've typically spent nine months of every year away from Ireland. So, put it another way, in the last decade, we've only spent at best two and a half years at home.

The second type of Westlife day is the tour day. This is much more fun. You get up at whatever time you like, literally! You haven't got a gig until the evening, so you can shop, see family, hang out or just relax, whatever, until about six. Then you head to catering, eat, chill out, get ready for the show and then hit the stage. Then it's back on the tour bus, over to your hotel or on to the next destination on the tour, lie in bed and usually look at the ceiling for about two hours because you can't go to sleep! That sort of day is a lot of fun, we love it.

The third type of day is a recording day. We don't usually like recording or singing before two o'clock, because your voice isn't awake before then. You can talk at ten o'clock in the morning but you can't really sing till two or three in the afternoon – that's what I find, anyway. Mark likes singing at five or six o'clock, he doesn't start till evening time. So I usually go in first and then Mark goes in and then the other two lads.

You might be in the studio till very late at night and there's often no one else about, so somehow it feels really secretive. It's always so exciting because you are actually making a record, you are hearing yourself sing, trying different things, putting a song together. Typically, that will take about eight weeks of the early summer.

Then the first single tends to get released in the autumn, and maybe another one a month or so later, then it's the album release and before you know it, you're back to promotion again.

By 2002, this routine was fairly well established, *adds Kian.* How those days played out over the course of a year was pretty set too: in January, it's fairly quiet but you might go off and do a bit of European promo; you start touring in February, March and play those shows up till the summer; then you have a few weeks off, although there's always a few summer shows; then in the second half of summer, you start recording a new album, begin the promo, shoot the videos, the photo shoots, all that stuff through August and September; then the album comes out and it's full blast through to Christmas. The market falls off on 18 December, roughly, then you have Christmas at home, then back to January and it all starts again!

For me personally, when it was announced that that year's album was going to be a greatest hits package, I felt it was a little premature. However, this was the way it went with boy bands ...

Nonetheless, we wanted to make it much more than just a reissue of old tracks, so we added six new songs and it felt like we were promoting a normal new album. And it did very well. It's our second bestselling album now, with over 1.5 million copies sold.

That was purely formula, *suggests Mark.* Three albums, *Greatest Hits*, bam, thanks a million, there you go. I think the *Greatest Hits* was probably premature, yes. The thing is, there is a technical formula that says when a boy band gets signed, the contract is for five albums; they do three and then the *Greatest Hits* comes out, leaving an album for any solo career. Some labels even discount any *Greatest Hits*, leaving two albums on the contract for two solo careers.

In interviews at the time of *Unbreakable: The Greatest Hits*, people were constantly asking us to 'squash the rumours' about splitting up. At the time I was like, 'Well, maybe Westlife will be over, who knows?' To be fair, most pop history confirms the formula I just explained. The very same history books will also tell you that most pop bands don't last very long after a *Greatest Hits* album.

Then the media reported that Shane had been offered a multi-million pound contract to go solo, *says Nicky*. The first I heard of it was when I read about it in the papers, so I immediately phoned Brian. Typically unexpected, his reaction was, 'Fair play to him in a way. You can't knock him if he wants to do that.' I was shocked and thought, *Fuck that, we're supposed to be a team. I'm not gonna be messed around like that!* I hate secrecy and if Shane had been offered a solo deal and, more importantly, if he wanted to have a go at one while Westlife was still going strong, then I wanted to know. And I wanted to know *now*. Then I spoke to Shane who told me straight away it was complete bullshit.

Even if I had been approached about a solo album, *confirms Shane*, it would have only ever been a one-word conversation: 'No.'

Not interested in any way.

Why would I be?

I'm in a great band with me mates. We travel the world, our gang, playing to thousands of people and selling millions of records. I'd be off me nut to leave that for a record that might not work. Maybe if we eventually called it a day all of us might look at our options, although even then I'm not sure it appeals. But as long as Westlife is together, it isn't gonna happen.

Think about it: no matter how big anyone's solo record was, it would have to be huge to beat what Westlife has achieved. Plus, I love singing on stage with my mates, the four of us up there having a great time. The tours are hilarious, we share so much. I can't imagine standing up on stage solo, or being on my own in the tour bus, all that. I'd be lonely, for Christ's sake!'

*   *   *

After the *Greatest Hits* album and tour, we didn't split up, *points out Nicky*. It was never gonna happen anyway, it was just something for the papers to talk about. Besides, there was no let up, it was straight into our fifth studio album.

We did feel slightly stale at that point, or at least that we were moving into uncharted waters. No one really expects a 'boy band' to go past the *Greatest Hits*, including us, so the fifth album as a band was something we wanted to get right. We were still selling out arenas, and one thing we refused to allow was the fans to feel short-changed. Nothing has ever been allowed to get in the way of our live shows being sensational – people spend their hard-earned money on tickets and there are no excuses, regardless of band circumstances, for the shows not being brilliant. The live side is up to us, the record label isn't involved, but obviously the nature of the live set depends on the album that precedes it.

So we got our heads together with Louis and Steve Mac and started making plans for the next record, which became *Turnaround*.

Despite feeling stale about the process, I think we bonded even more closely as a band. We were a little more on our own than we'd been used to, Simon Cowell was really busy with *American Idol* and his career, which was exploding.

For the first three years of our career, *explains Kian*, Simon was involved in every decision to do with the band – *every* decision. Obviously when *American Idol* and *X Factor* came along, that wasn't always possible.

Mark: Previously he used to come down to every rehearsal we had. He'd look at every jacket, every shirt, every tie, every pair of shoes, and it'd be like, 'Don't like those, love them, we need to get a bit more of this ...' Sonny Takhar was a huge part in that, too, very much so. But they had become so busy with Syco, Simon's TV production company, and all that media empire, that they obviously couldn't have that level of involvement anymore – I wouldn't have expected them to. Jesus, if I was Simon Cowell and I had all that, I wouldn't take time off to go and see what Westlife were wearing in a photo shoot, you know what I mean?!

Although the album had done well, *confesses Kian*, it was around the time of *Turnaround* that I found myself getting in too deep in terms of involvement with the record company side of things, specifically the song choices. It was the first album where I got intimately involved with the song choices – a big mistake.

You might think that sounds strange, but I'll tell you why.

We're not the main songwriters in Westlife. We've written songs for the band, as you know, but we have to rely on songwriters to provide us with material as well. So, conversations have to be had about song choices. In the case of the *Turnaround* album, I was being sent songs and I was sending them to the boys and we'd all chat about them.

Mark then came up with a song called 'Rainbow Zephyr', which was originally by a group called Relish, and we reworked this into an up-tempo tune that seemed ideal for Westlife. Eventually, this track morphed into 'Hey Whatever' and we loved it, we really pushed for it to be the first single off the new album.

Then we got a call from Simon Cowell. He wanted to talk to us in his office about the album. He sat behind his desk and calmly said, 'You don't have your hit here. You just don't have your hit.'

'Well, what do you think of "Hey Whatever"?'

'It's alright,' he replied.

We were still determined so we put 'Hey Whatever' out as a single. So we pushed and we pushed and that's what happened. Now, as you know from that heady moment in Pete Waterman's studio when we were tipped off about our first number 1, on the Tuesday of every week that we release a single, I get a phone call from Louis Walsh around about half-eight, with the midweek. This time was no different.

'Kian,' said Louis, 'it's at number 4,' our worst midweek position ever, 'and Simon wants to see you all in his office at 11 o'clock.'

To be fair, by many successful bands' standards, that was a great position to be in, but relative to Westlife's previous chart history, it was seen as a disaster.

I recall ringing the other boys and telling them about the meeting, and as I dialled each of their numbers, I was thinking, *Fuck, fuck, fuck, it's only number 4.*

I should give some context here, *says Shane*. We had already had 11 number 1 singles and although 'Bop Bop Baby' had only got to number 5, it had sold over 110,000 copies. 'Hey Whatever' was the only single not to reach 100,000 sales, stalling at just under 80,000.

When we arrived at the record company's offices, *continues Kian*, I was chatting to some people I knew in the International Department on the fifth floor just prior to going into our meeting. Then someone came up to me and, in hushed tones, said, 'Kian, they're blaming you. You were involved in the song choices and you wanted this as a single. They're saying it's your fault.'

Suddenly, a big crashing pressure descended on me. I sat down and I actually recall feeling the biggest weight pushing down on my shoulders that I'd ever felt in my life. My first reaction was, 'Why blame me?' After all, I felt I'd also done a lot to orchestrate the album and ease its making, but that clearly wasn't the talking point.

We walked into Simon's office and I just sat there pretty quietly. I was gutted.

Simon's office walls are covered in discs and awards, *explains Nicky*, and he sits behind a huge desk, smoking like a steam train. Behind him is a massive mirror engraved with the words 'Yes, Simon, you do look terrific.'

We all sat down, waiting to hear what he had to say, *remembers Kian*. Simon said, 'I have a song I'd like you to hear, boys. I think we should put this out as the next single,' and as he spoke, he pressed play on his machine.

Barry Manilow's 'Mandy' came out of the speakers.

'I want it to be the next single and I believe it will be a huge hit,' he said. 'Trust me, lads, trust me.'

It was the next single.

It was Record of the Year.

After that, I just backed away from the music choices. That day in the record company offices, with all those comments and the bad chart position, I just thought, *Fuck that, I'm in way too deep. I'm 23 years of age and I'm fucking about with a major record label and trying to make a decision that I don't know enough about.*

The happy middle ground I've now reached works well for me: I still get all the songs and I still chat for hours with the boys about our preferences, but me personally, I tend not to involve myself with the record company debates about song choices.

* * *

Sometimes, the madness of our jobs can be put into very sharp perspective in an instant, *explains Nicky*. You can easily get all fixated on what chart position you are, how many albums have you sold, how good or bad is a certain review. It's your job, so you have a certain pride in that. Then something comes along and crunches everything into perspective.

In late 2003, we travelled to India for the very first MTV India Awards. You might think that seeing that deprived country was the slap of reality, but actually it was more to do with something that happened to one of our crew.

India is a big market and we hadn't been there before, so we were well up for the trip. The second we stepped off the plane in Mumbai, it was a severe culture shock. The poverty was shocking. We'd read about it, but seeing it for ourselves was a rude awakening. The airport was slime-infested and, remember, we'd been travelling the world in private jets and helicopters for some time. I remember the police officers were really aggressive; they had these huge sticks and just seemed very confrontational.

We then travelled to Goa to shoot a video, a place that is the main holiday resort in India. We had a bit of fun on some jet-skis and down on the beach, you know, a bit of craic. When the shoot was all done and dusted, we headed back for these awards. The bus we were on drove through the most abject poverty I have ever seen: hardly any solid roads, cows wandering across the traffic, people sitting in the gutter, rubbish piled up everywhere. We even saw people living under motorway bridges. It was awful. I hate saying this, but it was like something out of Michael Jackson's 'Thriller' video, people emerging from the dark shadows under a motorway bridge. Very frightening ...

Which is a shame, because I loved India, *says Mark*. It was an amazing experience and I'd love to go back ...

We were staying in probably the only three-star hotel in the area, *continues Nicky*, which had 24-hour armed guards outside. The hotel was on a hill, so it felt almost like we were in a fort. When we went to rehearsals, the armed guards followed us.

We had a signing arranged and when we got there, we were surprised to see them shut the road off completely – because several thousand fans had turned up. It was absolute chaos. We were just sitting there, trying to sign these records and chat happily with the fans, while outside was mayhem and we could see that the police were very heavy-handed. The pandemonium was too much after a very short while and they told us they were going to cut the signing short for safety reasons. Then, when it came to leaving, they beat a path through the crowds and we were instructed to run to the coach. It was pretty unsettling stuff.

We went from there to the final rehearsals. The stage was outdoors and we could barely sing for the flies buzzing around our faces and the incredible heat. I thought at that point that the trip couldn't get much worse. But it did.

As we jumped down from the stage, we noticed Lasty, our security man of five years, literally on his hands and knees crying. Lasty was a big fella, covered in tattoos and a very tough man, so this was a really bizarre thing to see, especially in the middle of all this Indian madness. He was a big softie underneath, but you really didn't expect to see this.

I said, 'Lasty, what's wrong?' and he told me that he'd just received a voicemail from his mate at home to say his father had collapsed and he was very poorly, to call home immediately as he didn't actually know if he was going to be OK or not.

We tried to reassure Lasty that his dad would be fine and all got into our cars to go back to the hotel. I sat in the back with Kian and Lasty was in the front with the Indian driver.

'Where did your mate say he collapsed?'

Lasty told us it was by a local shop.

'OK, well, let's start from scratch. We'll find out all the hospitals near to that shop and phone round ...' We were just trying to calm him down and do something useful.

Then his mate rang him back and told him that his dad was dead.

Lasty just exploded with grief. He threw his phone across the dashboard and tried to get out of the moving car. Kian and me lunged at him and managed to grab him before he opened the door properly and we dragged him back in. He was sobbing and screaming and we both just held on to him as tightly as we could. It was really distressing to see. He'd lost his mam some years earlier and his dad, Dennis, was basically his best mate. It turned out he'd suffered a massive heart attack.

It was horrible.

We got Lasty to the airport and booked him a first-class ticket home. Unfortunately, the flight wasn't till four in the morning and it was only six in the evening then, so Lasty had to sit in the airport departure lounge for hours waiting to go home.

That was a low point, that trip. Not because of the country and the fans, because they were brilliant. But it holds too many sad memories. I have to say it was appalling. I don't think I was right for a while when we came home after that. I kind of sunk in to a little bit of a depression. It was Christmas and that trip was our last promo before the festive break. It took a lot out of all of us.

Talk about perspective.

10 Years of Westlife...

What can i say
they have been the
best years of my
life and it is all
because of you
reading this.

CHAPTER SIXTEEN

BRIAN

Shane: When Brian McFadden told us he was leaving Westlife, I thought we were being punk'd.

It was a massive shock to us all, there's no denying that. I absolutely thought we were being punk'd. Nicky actually checked him for TV mics. I was literally waiting for the camera crew to burst in.

But they didn't.

Brian was serious.

He was leaving Westlife.

He'd told us a few times before that he was leaving the band, *explains Kian.* But we just put it down to Brian being Brian. He was like that. He'd say, 'I really fancy a moped,' and he'd just go out, there and then, and buy one. Remember when we bought those three Ferraris and Brian had the canary yellow one? He was the sort of character who'd buy the first house he walked into, the first car he sat in. He was impulsive, energetic – that's what was so great about him. So when he'd first mentioned this before, we hadn't actually taken it seriously, to be perfectly honest with you.

He'd told me in a taxi some time before, *admits Mark*. Though I have to be honest, I couldn't remember it. He later said it'd been in a taxi after we'd had a drunken night out together. We used to go out partying quite a lot, Brian and me, and we'd drink and stumble home and things got forgotten like any friends who go out partying. Maybe I was too drunk that night, I don't know, but I don't remember him saying those things to me. If he says he did, then he did, but I just couldn't remember them.

Perhaps, like everyone else, I just dismissed it as one of the things Brian said. There was no logic for him to leave Westlife. Apart from our obvious huge success, his own specific role in the band had never been bigger. On the *Turnaround* album, he'd sung more songs and more brilliantly than ever before. His public profile was also very big, due to the massive press coverage of his wedding and a photo shoot in *OK!* magazine.

We'd done the promotion for 'Mandy', *explains Kian*, and then had the festive break. The first thing we did when we got back after Christmas was a ChildLine concert in Ireland. We went out to a club afterwards with all the band and Louis as well, and he said to Louis then that he wanted to leave Westlife. I remember it being passed around the band in the noise of that club but, again, no one took it that seriously. Not in any disrespectful way, just, 'It's Brian being Brian, you know.' That was our general attitude again.

Next up was the Meteor Awards a few nights later, a big Irish music event. We'd won several awards so we were all having a tipple backstage afterwards. Brian was drunk, like the rest of us, and again he said he wanted to leave the band. We were in the dressing room when he said it and when I replied, 'Ah, don't be silly,' he said, 'Lads, I'm serious,' and walked off and left the venue. We had some press photo calls to do after, so we hauled Louis up with us so that no one suspected anything was wrong.

The next day was the first day of rehearsals for the forthcoming *Turnaround* tour. Brian showed up, but it was slow progress. We only learned one routine that day, so as we were wrapping up, I turned to Brian and said, 'Look, Brian, what's the craic? There's obviously an issue here. You've told us a few times now that you want to leave the band, should we not sit down and talk about it?'

Very calmly, he said, 'Yes, that'd be good.'

We arranged to meet at the serviced apartments we'd all rented during the rehearsals. We all sat down when Brian arrived and said, 'Right, come on, what's the story?'

'I'm hanging up my boots, lads.'

Even though we'd all heard this before, this time we could see he meant it, *remembers Shane*. It was such a shock, that's why I thought we were on MTV being punk'd. My mind was a whirl. I couldn't comprehend that he would want to leave. He enjoyed so much about Westlife and he was a great fella, he'd literally give you the last shirt off his back if he thought it would help you. He was our joker, the jester, the madcap ball of energy. So to be sitting there deadly serious, telling us he was leaving Westlife, it was just very surreal.

We sat there for only about 40 minutes and talked about it, *continues Kian*. I couldn't believe he had the balls to leave. It was a *huge* decision.

At first, we tried to convince him otherwise. There was no animosity, no shouting; it was all very calm and respectful, just a quiet conversation between the five of us. Nicky even suggested that we went to counselling as a band.

He wasn't interested, he was definitely leaving, *says Shane*, but he said that if it helped matters, he was happy to do the tour – which was starting in just a couple of weeks' time.

We didn't think that was a good idea, so it was agreed he wouldn't do the tour, he'd leave.

So he did. He got up, gave us all a hug and left.

As Brian clicked the door shut and left, *admits Kian*, I just kept thinking, *The band's over, the band's over, the band's over ...*

We didn't know what the fuck to do, *says Nicky*. First off, we rang Louis and told him, and he said he was coming straight over. He'd be about half an hour, so in the meantime three of us said we'd go and tell our girlfriends.

My reaction wasn't really what you might expect, *recalls Mark*. For about half an hour after he told us, I almost had a sense of relief coming over me. Everyone was reacting in their own individual way, Kian was saying, 'This is it lads, it's over,' they were talking about it and I was just listening to all this and thinking, *Maybe it is over, maybe this is finished now, maybe this is the right time for this to finish.*

The lads all went off to tell their girlfriends and wives while we waited for Louis to arrive, so I just went to my room and sat there alone, thinking it all through. Being very open with you, I even thought to myself, *OK, now I can go back to Sligo, I can go back to that life I had that I cherished so much and worried about losing. I can go and see my family and friends.* There was definitely a sense of relief that this brilliant lunacy was all over.

I phoned Gillian and chatted about it, *explains Shane*, then I sat in my hotel room and I remember thinking, *What could possibly be that wrong? Why on Earth would you want to leave Westlife?* But clearly there were other issues as well, probably stuff we didn't know about and he never talked about and didn't want to talk about, which is fair enough.

I'd arranged to meet Louis halfway in my car, *says Nicky*, and show him where the apartments were, but I was so muddled up in my mind I got lost. I was driving around parts of Dublin that I knew like the back of my hand, but I was lost. Eventually I found the street we'd arranged to meet in – a few minutes away from the apartments – and waited for Louis' car to pull up.

When Louis came into the room to meet the four of us, *recounts Kian*, he was amazing. He sat us down and said simply, 'This isn't the end. It isn't over, boys. We aren't going to let this affect us. You're still going to go on tour, you'll make more records, Westlife will continue and be as big as ever – *bigger*!'

Within a few minutes of Louis arriving, we were so hyped up about rehearsals and continuing as a four-piece, it was incredible.

The very next day the four of us showed up at rehearsals, absolutely raring to go.

We'd organized a press conference to officially announce Brian's departure. Again, Louis was very positive. He refused to try to hide it, he just wanted it all out in the open. He wanted to do the conference and get on with the rest of Westlife's future. He was so calm and collected about it and so passionate about continuing undeterred, it was hard for that not to rub off on us.

The press conference was at the Four Seasons hotel in Dublin. It was packed when we all walked out to face the media. Brian sat on the end and explained that he felt it was time to leave, that he couldn't commit enough time to his family if he stayed and that he wanted to be with his kids and wife more.

Then I read out a letter. The rest of the boys didn't want me to, they said I should just write the letter and give it to Brian in private, but I really wanted to do it. It was very emotional and I actually welled up, I got kinda teary reading it out, I was short of breath, tearful. Then we all hugged, the conference was over and that was it.

Brian was officially, publicly, no longer in Westlife.

We went and did a photo call as a four-piece. We had already announced we were still doing the tour and moving forward.

As far as I was aware, Brian wanted to leave the band to be with his wife and family. Obviously he was unhappy. I think maybe he was unhappy in his life and perhaps he associated that unhappiness more with Westlife than anything else. So he became unhappy doing Westlife.

Right from the start, I'd had a great relationship with Brian. When Westlife went to Dublin for those three or four months we were rehearsing for record companies, I lived with Brian. I stayed in his house with his family and got to know them very well and we became very close. Me and Brian used to go out partying together; we got on really, really well away from the band. In the band, we didn't necessarily get on as well because he was this wild, energetic, hundred miles an hour type. You couldn't get him to focus his attention for too long on something before he'd move on to the next thing. For instance, he seriously loved his music and if he'd heard a new tune, he'd play you, say, 30 seconds of it and then say, 'Yeah, but listen to this tune as well,' then play 30 seconds of something else and then say, 'No, no, no, hold on, this one's better,' before you'd really had a chance to hear anything. As a friend, I loved him to pieces for that and got on with him great, but in the band he was a heartache for me. I was dealing with Louis and the record company and I was trying to get Brian to do things and he always didn't want to do them, so ... We didn't really clash as such, but he became a wee bit hard work for me – and to be perfectly fair, I became hard work for him too, because we were both pulling in opposite directions.

There were specific musical issues too. When we'd started writing our own material for *World of our Own*, Brian had very strong ideas about how he wanted his songs to sound. That wasn't always possible and I think it kind of affected him a wee bit. He loved the *Turnaround* album, he felt it was the best record we'd made, but then he was disappointed that we released 'Mandy'. There is a song called 'On my Shoulder', a much more complex track by Steve Mac and Wayne Hector, that Brian absolutely loved and really wanted as a single. We'd had the conversations about singles and 'Mandy', and some of us were genuinely concerned about our careers, but Brian wasn't, he was like, 'Come on, let's just put this out, let's release great music!'

So I knew he was unhappy with the band, that was clear, but I didn't think it was terminal. We'd all had phases when we hadn't agreed with the song choices, and all sorts of decisions might be taken that go against what you'd prefer, but that is the nature of being in a band with five people.

For a brief while, *muses Mark*, I felt really guilty because I thought that he'd perhaps been looking to confide in me and talk to me about his concerns, and I'd not even remembered what he'd said. I know now, though, that his mind had already been made up and the chat in the taxi had made no difference to his decision.

Me and Brian had a lot of things in common: the record-business marketing machine rubbed both of us up the wrong way a lot of the time and we tended to sit by each other in big meetings, we both liked a cigarette, we both loved to jam and to sing out harmonies, and neither of us was particularly good at getting up in the mornings! We spent a good deal of time together and I was very, very sad when he left.

I think people's happiness is more important than Westlife. Even though I cannot be any more passionate about the band than I am, it's just a band at the end of the day and if it's making you unhappy, it can't be allowed to do that. Something has to change to stop that unhappiness. In Brian's case, he couldn't see any change being enough, I guess. We could never justify keeping someone in the band if they were unhappy.

Brian was the other Dubliner in the band, *says Nicky*, and at the very beginning we would have been closest to each other. We were from a more suburban city life, so we gelled. I like him a lot. Brian's personality is so quick, and he is generous and would help you in any way. There was a lot of hurt when he left. It was very quick and very shocking and, yes, I was worried about my career too.

But I've tried to be very careful about what I said in the media, we've been through too much together for any throwaway comment to affect that. For a long time, the interviews were all 'Brian, Brian, Brian, will he come back?' People were looking for headlines. But if I have ever said anything he's not liked in the press, it was never intended.

He was one of the lads, and we share some fantastic memories of each other; when he left, something else left with him. However, we've worked hard and now there's a new magic with us *four*. But, Brian, from the heart, thank you for those fantastic years.

It's easy now to reflect, *continues Kian*, and suggest that Brian's marriage to Kerry came too early on. It didn't impact on the band professionally at all really, but within the other four members, we were worried about him. We worried it was all going too fast; it seemed like he was married with kids before you knew it. But to be fair, that was always Brian – everything was so fast, that's his nature. He had the world at his feet. That was just his way and, to be fair, who am I to correct him anyway? You've got to love him for that, he's a fantastic character. I cared about him and I tried – we all tried – to slow things down. We didn't want to see anyone make mistakes in life, especially someone who was that close to us. He was a great guy to be on the road with, a great guy to hang out with, a great guy to go to the casino with. He loved playing cards, he loved his music, he was this big, bubbly personality. For me, there were never any personal issues with Brian, only ones to do with the band.

At first, he helped us get a record deal because our sound was so full with that extra bass harmony and visually we then had the dynamics right. Regardless of what ultimately happened, at the end of the day Brian spent years on the road with us and was a big part of all those early stories, and you can't forget what he contributed to the band's success. It's perhaps easy to overlook that, because we went on as a four and it worked so well, it went on to bigger things, but we still need to recognize what Brian McFadden did for Westlife.

In the jacuzzi on holiday.

MARK xx

Our first holiday, summer '05

With Kevin on a boat trip in Asia.

Saffy.

With Mum and Dad at a wedding.

With Maria in Capri.

Sunset dinner by the Andaman Sea, anyone?

With both Nanas on the day we were given the keys to the city.

New Year's Eve in Sligo with best mates. Left–right: Lynchy, Rowen, Jason, me

Backstage at a roadshow in the USA with Beyoncé.

A fairytale in France, August 9, 2003.

Nicky

How lucky am I? ... Georgina's stunning.

My dad, my best mate and my inspiration.

My nana, Lily, my biggest fan.

Ireland's best Taoiseach.

The wedding party.

rolling to our first dance.

Under the wing.

Gggrrr!!! Me and Rocco.

Our engagement picture – she said 'Yes!'

I could stay like this all day ... me with Jay at home, October 2007.

Seasons in the sun ... first thought, Where's the gym?

Double whammy! Rocco and Jay singing and performing already!

Me and Nicole asleep in our bed in Castledale in Sligo (3 weeks old). She likes her sleep, like her Daddy!

Me, Gillian and Nicole on holiday in Mauritius 2007.

Me and Gill celebrating St Patrick's Day on tour in Manchester, 2007.

Going to Shay Given's charity ball in 2006.

Getting ready as Sgt Pepper for Nicky's 21st, in fancy dress.

Swimming with dolphins in Mexico.

In the Maldives on honeymoon.

Kissing outside
the church on our
wedding day.

Nicole's first time on stage at
The Point Depot in Dublin, my
proudest moment on stage.

Our wedding party
inside the church.

My immediate family on my 21st birthday
at Lillie's Bordello in Dublin

Me with my
mates, Keith,
Paul and Brig.

Jumping from 13,000 feet.

The surf crew taking the mick in Morrocco.

On holiday with Jodi in Hawaii.

On a nice one in Majorca.

With our best
buddies, Jason and
Ciara on their
wedding day.

Mine and Jodi's families.

With Ozzy.

Me and my little boy, Prince.

Hitting the waves with my brother Tom, his
wife Julie, my little brother Colm and Jodi.

On our first holiday together in Barbados.

In Las Vegas
winning a
World Music
Award.

PART III

CHAPTER SEVENTEEN

'ALL THE BEST BANDS ARE GANGS'

Westlife has always been a gang, *states Shane*. That's our mentality. We were like that from Day One and so when Brian left, you might think that close-knit gang vibe would crumble.

Far from it. We were never stronger.

It was amazing, in the face of him leaving, the press conference, the speculation in the media about our future, all that stuff, we were just *totally* focused, the four fucking musketeers. That episode made us close ranks like you wouldn't believe. We were strong with Brian in the band, but after he left we were impenetrable.

There wasn't a negative vibe towards Brian, but we were very pragmatic about it. We felt that if he wanted to leave, if he wanted to take that gamble with his life, that was fine, that was totally his choice, his decision, and you had to respect him for that, so we let him go in peace and try to stop being unhappy. I wouldn't knock the fella to this day.

But we weren't going to let it fuck up our lives, no way.

We just weren't going to let his decision affect the four of our lives and the four of our futures, our kids' futures and our families' futures, no way.

Literally, in that two-week window when we rehearsed for the *Turnaround* tour, we grew closer than ever before. It was the most amazing feeling of strength and focus. We rehearsed so intensely and in between working that out, we would talk and say stuff like, 'We're tighter now. We're not going to let anyone get in between us ever. No one's going to come within a mile of breaking this up.' We became, overnight really, ultra-protective of what we had, what we had worked for. Having seen how easily that could be swept away, we weren't prepared to let that happen.

We felt like fucking comrades.

Shane's absolutely right, *agrees Kian*. We had just two weeks to get organized in those rehearsals. So we quickly rechoreographed the dance moves and tweaked the set and then nailed it. There was no messing.

The first night on stage without Brian in the band was in Belfast – and I have to tell you, it was one of the best shows we've ever done. There was tons of press interest. Industry guests and fans were all curious to see how we'd perform as a four-piece. It was pretty intense.

We knew we were ready. I have to say, a key person in making that happen was Priscilla Samuels, our choreographer since Day One. When Brian left, she just fired in and reorganized us, got it all sorted in double-quick time. She's a very dominant woman – no one ever dares answer back to her! But she commands your respect. Likewise, she will constantly say, 'Respect your audience, respect your stage, respect what you have.' She was brilliant in those frantic two weeks of rehearsals for giving us all a buzz again. She still does it to this day.

We nailed that first gig and the reviews were almost universally positive, the journos loved it, the fans loved it and we got a sense that people admired us and respected for taking Brian's departure on the chin, not cancelling the tour and just getting on with it. The tour was brilliant and Brian even came to see a show himself. We absolutely nailed that tour.

The tour was brilliant, as Kian says, *adds Mark*. For me, having struggled with my confidence for so long, it means everything to me that people like what I sing on stage. If someone says, 'You sang crap, but the stage looked gorgeous,' I'd be gutted. That's not the right way round.

Rehearsals were a bit scary and a bit rushed and panicky, but we were so focused that we could have dealt with anything that was thrown at us at that point in time. We were so determined, it was almost a super-human focus. We were going to be ready for the first show and we were going to be fucking brilliant, and that was all that mattered.

Louis played a key role in convincing us that we could go on without Brian and, in fact, could be bigger and more successful even. We decided to buy into that thought and believe it and embrace that idea. As soon as we did that, we had something to prove to the public, something to prove to ourselves. We were ready to go again.

No journalist was going to go home from that gig without enjoying it and thinking it was brilliant and no manager, no record company executive, no fan, *nobody* would be disappointed by what

Westlife was like without Brian. It was probably one of the most important couple of weeks in our whole career. It proved we could rise to the occasion when we had to. When backed into a corner, we come out fighting.

When Brian left, there was a huge pressure on us to perform well. But that tour was a massive success in every way. It was our biggest tour ever and it was the cleanest, tightest, most polished set of gigs we've ever done. It was pretty flawless. It really did certify in everyone's minds that Westlife was still really good without Brian, in fact better. We totally pulled it out of the bag.

I kept thinking about all those years before, *says Kian*, when Louis had said, 'We need five in the band, because one of you might leave and that way we'd still having a working band of four.' That's what he always said from Day One.

Oddly enough, before he left, we had a certain anonymity to a lot of people, our names weren't necessarily known, it was more 'yer man from Westlife'. I actually think after Brian left, that helped us, I really do. When Robbie left Take That, they didn't last long, because he was such a well-known personality; when Geri Halliwell left the Spice Girls, likewise. We were different back then. Every time you'd see us on TV, we were with Westlife. You still don't tend to see us on TV on our own. There's the odd time, like when I did the *X-Factor* with Louis, but 99 per cent of the time, it's the band. So to some outsiders, when Brian split, it was a case of 'yer man from Westlife' has left. A lot of people didn't know our individual names at that stage, and I honestly think that helped us regroup and stamp our personalities over Westlife for the future.

*   *   *

Just over six months after Brian left Westlife, he released a solo album, *states Kian*. He also split up with Kerry. We'd heard he was working on a solo record, but we didn't know for sure. The single came out and went to number 1 and initially the album did quite well.

For my part, I didn't react too positively to these developments. He told me he was leaving Westlife to be with his family. Now, I love Brian to pieces, I respect him for leaving Westlife when he was unhappy, I respect him for leaving a marriage he was unhappy in, I respect him for doing what he wanted to do with music and taking such a risk. Being a member of Westlife is not for everybody, and to this day I think fair play to Brian for doing it as long as he did, for making that massive contribution and dedicating as much of his life to the band as he did.

Around about 2007, we had a few negative words with each other, something which, I'm happy to say, seems resolved now. Let me explain.

For years and years and years, we'd been asked, 'How are things with Brian?' and we'd always spoken very highly of him and very nicely. However, by that year, I found myself getting a wee bit more honest about it. What I'm about to say here is nothing I haven't said in private conversation with Brian. I felt like he laughed at me in the press conference. Now I know he has a nervous laugh and a nervous energy to him, and he's explained to me that's all it was. That may be, but it made me feel strange that I thought I was being laughed at when I was actually very emotional and reading out that letter. Brian has said to me and also in interviews that perhaps I was emotional because I thought the band was over. Maybe that's not massively untrue, I probably did think the band was going to break up, but I was still sad to see him go, do you know what I mean? He was our mate.

I've since said that we shouldn't have done the press conference and I stand by that. I think we glorified Brian too much when he left the band. I do think that looking back – as a business decision for Westlife – we made a very big deal about Brian leaving the band and that was probably unnecessary. In a way, that helped prepare the ground for his solo career. The shoe could very much be on the other foot now, Westlife could be down the tubes and he could be the next Robbie Williams, but it hasn't worked that way for him, not yet anyway. I really wish it had worked for both of us. I'd have loved him to have written his own material and become massive while Westlife were still doing their thing too. That would have been brilliant.

Anyway, some of these negative feelings of mine started trickling out in the press and Brian was obviously unhappy with them because he started texting Louis and Mark, asking why we were saying nasty things about him.

Eventually, I picked up the phone and spoke to him direct. We were great, great mates and I wanted to finally talk to him about it all. I remember saying, 'Don't be bothering sending these text messages. If you've got a problem with what I had to say in an interview, say it to me right here on the phone.' He explained his feelings and I explained mine.

Looking back on that call, I have to say I respect him for standing up for himself. Even though we didn't necessarily agree, he wanted to know why I was saying things he didn't like. He knows I'm the type of person to express my true feelings; I'm not afraid of saying what I think. I'm very glad he spoke to me in the way he did and that we had that conversation and sorted out our feelings. To this day, we remain great friends.

I personally think Brian left, *says Mark*, because he didn't want to be in Westlife anymore, simple as that. Spending more time with his family was a benefit of that. In time it became clear that his relationship with Kerry was in jeopardy and perhaps he wanted to spend time working on that marriage, but I don't think that's why he left the band, I'm not of that opinion.

There's also this expectation that celebrities have all the answers and, remember, we were still in our mid-twenties back then. Brian was just working things out in his head like any man with marriage issues and work problems, it was just that it was played out very publicly.

I don't blame him or hold anything against him, I have to say that, I really don't. I don't think he could have really ruined my career by leaving the band. We don't see as much of each now as we used to, obviously, because back then he was in the band and we saw each other every minute of every day sometimes, now he lives in Australia. You can't go from living in someone's pocket to being on the other side of the world without it affecting your relationship. What is nice is that when I do see Brian, I don't feel that I need to start getting to know him again, we just click and carry on as before. Ultimately, there are only five people in the world who know what it was like to be in Westlife during those years and that's a bond that will never be broken.

I still have the greatest respect for Brian. I'm grateful to him – just as I am grateful to the other three – for giving such commitment and dedication to the band, because that band has played such a big part in my life. Obviously, the others have continued to give that commitment and have really set their stall out in terms of effort and dedication, and what a team we have become as a result. But I don't have a bad thought in my body about Brian. He'll always be a very good friend of mine and I'll always have a big love for him.

I still see Brian, *says Shane*, but obviously not as much. We've been out for meals with him and Delta, we talk on the phone sometimes and we get on great. It's like going to college with someone and having a brilliant time with them for five years and then going on to work for different companies on different sides of the world – you'll always get on, there'll always be a bond. It's like that. I'll always have good feelings for Brian, he's done nothing against any of us, a great fella, I'll always respect him. I also know that we'll never be in a band together again. That's just a fact of life.

*   *   *

Brian leaving was our first big shock, *continues Shane*. It's enough of a shock to kill most bands, finish 'em. How many times have you seen one member leave and the band carries on, only to fall apart within a year or so? We just thought, *Why should it be like that? We aren't gonna let that happen*. I think it helped that we hadn't lost our lead singer. Brian had a great voice, don't get me wrong, and his contribution was brilliant. But it wasn't like if Ronan Keating had left Boyzone. Myself and Mark are perceived to be the 'lead' singers in Westlife, if there is such a thing, so when Brian left we were able to work around it. That's the way I saw it, the way Mark saw it, Kian and Nicky too.

By becoming closer as a unit behind the scenes, I definitely think we became much better on stage. We had to up the ante, our individual personalities had to come out more up there. We literally had to fill more of the stage too. And during that *Turnaround* tour, Westlife rose to that challenge and we ended up a far superior band at the end of it all. If we can survive that and then go on to have more huge success with our subsequent albums, then we can survive anything.

MARK xx   Kian   Shane   Nicky

CHAPTER EIGHTEEN

WHILE WE ARE BEING FRANK ...

'Right, guys, you've lost a member, you've lost a harmony, we need to change things around a little bit. You need to come back with something big. I think we should do a Rat Pack album.'

We were in Simon Cowell's office, *recalls Nicky*, and he was explaining what he thought should be our next record. We were all aware of the classic songs and performers from the Rat Pack period and we all liked the material, but it wasn't necessarily something we'd have thought of doing ourselves.

There's an old saying in the music business: 'You're only as good as your last album.' You might think certain bands, certain levels of success, exclude you from that, but our album of Rat Pack songs certainly made me feel this was a risk we were running.

Simon was confident. 'I think you're at a point in your career,' he said, 'where you can all step up to the plate a little bit. You're well known enough to be able to take this gamble, this risk. It'll be great.'

Robbie had had such a big success with it, so we thought, *We'll give it a shot.*

Recording that record was one of the funniest times ever in the studio – I remember thinking *Brian would have loved making this album* – and, later, it was one of the hardest for me personally. Initially, it was hilarious. In the first few years, we'd always be in the studio all together; you'd go up and do your vocals for an hour while the rest of the band were on the Play Station. This had changed over the years and we were spending more individual time recording, so you might get two weeks away before you were needed again. I felt it was losing some of the gang vibe, the craic, but at the same time, in Westlife you can't complain about time off!

Well, for the Rat Pack album – which was actually going to be called *Allow Us to Be Frank* – we recaptured much of that gang feeling again. We researched the songs and the period heavily. We all went to see a musical based on that genre and era. Me and Shane actually went to a musical in Las Vegas as well. We bought all the records, read books about them, did a proper job on it.

We didn't know at first who was going to sing what, that's why we all went to the studio together. It was so funny. The first two weeks we sang, it was just a load of really bad Elvis and Sinatra impersonations, all in the dodgiest American accents you've ever heard. We knew Elvis wasn't anywhere near Rat Pack, of course, but we just ended up sounding like him for some reason! We were killing ourselves laughing. It was great fun.

It took a while to settle into the songs and sing them with our own personalities, rather than a cabaret version. Then we gradually started to nail the songs. Shane first, then Mark, then over time we all got a feel for what was needed and really put in some good performances.

The one very fond memory I have of the Rat Pack album, *recalls Mark*, is how much of an enjoyable experience it was to be singing such different songs. I didn't look at it like I was trying to copy Frank Sinatra or Dean Martin, I was just giving my own take on it. A seasoned Rat Pack fan probably wouldn't have liked my vocals on the album, because I didn't sound like those singers, but I felt that distinction was important. I love to vary things and I love versatility, so as a singer I definitely liked recording the album.

It also made me *really* appreciate Frank Sinatra's voice. I knew of his vocals and I liked them, but once we did the research and got involved in the songs, it made you realize he had such an amazing voice. It's interesting what his voice does to you when you listen to it. It isn't about high notes or vocal gymnastics, it's just a pure, solid gold voice.

Unfortunately, at the end of all these fantastically enjoyable sessions, *remembers Nicky*, I ended up having a bit of a disagreement with the producer, Steve Mac, because of certain vocals of mine that weren't used in the final mix. Because it was Rat Pack, there were no real harmonies, it was all pretty much lead vocals, so on some songs I wasn't singing at all. I spoke to the other boys about it. They totally understood where I was coming from. It was nothing to do with the lads. Let me explain. I'm not the type of person to just pick up the cheque – forget that – so I wanted to ask Steve what the story was, but the lads, knowing my personality, thought it would be best if someone else did it for me, so I wouldn't 'rock the boat', a saying which I despise. If I've got something to say, I prefer to be honest and say it.

Shane kindly had a word with Steve Mac for me, trying to work it out. He's a legend of a producer, but I had to feel like I'd had my say about the vocals. Steve just kept saying, 'Well, I've got to put the best foot forward for the band.' That was absolutely his duty as producer, I guess, but I was looking at how this would impact on us later: 'The thing is, Steve, can you see why I'd be uncomfortable when we promote and tour this record and Mark and Shane are singing "Ain't That a Kick in the Head" and I'm just standing there?' At the same time, I was keen not to rock the boat, so it was a tricky balance.

We were doing a TV show called *She's the One* in Manchester, where we picked a girl to come and sing with us on the album ...

... and we did three big auditions around the UK, *recalls Kian*, where we all sat at a table, *X Factor* style, and fans came up and sang to us without any backing music. The girl who won was very good, she stood out a mile ...

... and while we were on a bus journey for this film, *continues Nicky*, the final mixes of the new album came through. I couldn't see that much had changed. I could sense the lads listening anxiously to see what vocals the mixes were using. I wasn't happy. 'I've broken my bollocks singing all day on these songs, you've all done your best for me, Louis has done his best for me, there's nothing here to do.' So I flew home that day and said, 'I've had enough of this. Lads, until this changes, I'm at home.'

It sounds pretty dramatic, but in reality I don't think I was ever going to leave the band. It would have to be something pretty disastrous to make me leave Westlife. Louis called me in Dublin that night and he was great, he understood where I was coming from. I just couldn't face doing the whole tour and all the promo, just standing there while Shane and Mark sang their parts. The boys agreed and wanted to use more of my vocals, even at the expense of their own. I have to say, through this whole tricky patch, the boys and Louis were first class.

Shane had told Steve that I was going home and was extremely annoyed. So I decided to call Steve Mac. I was driving up to a spa in Northern Ireland with Georgina to take a break to get away from it all, but I phoned him on the three-hour journey. I like Steve Mac, I like him a lot, he's a nice guy, he's a very funny guy and I still think he is a very good guy to work with, but at that moment I had to stand up for what I believed in and he rightly had to stand up for what he believed in. To be fair to Steve, he pulled no punches and I like that in someone as I am exactly the same.

'I have to put the best foot forward for the record,' he repeated, 'otherwise I feel I'm not doing my job properly.'

I said, 'But the best foot forward for the continuation of the band might be something different though, Steve. If I'm not in there, then I don't know where I go from here.'

After about an hour talking very honestly with each other, he agreed to use more of my vocals.

That was a difficult time for me in Westlife. I'd never put a gun to the lads' heads and I'd never walk away from this band unless something absolutely catastrophic happened – we're far too close for that, as mates as much as anything else. But there are certain things that need to be there to make that clock keep ticking – for all of us – and that's why I felt very dark towards the end of those sessions.

Recording can be tough and, to be honest, sometimes it can wear you down, but I've always believed you've got to fight for what you believe is right.

*　　*　　*

Allow Us to Be Frank was not a number 1 album, hitting number 3 instead, *says Shane*. It sold just over 700,000 copies, which is a lot, but it's also less than half what four of our nine albums have done and it remains our worst-selling album. It was way short of the million mark in the UK, obviously, which to us felt like a blow.

I think we pulled it off, that Rat Pack album, *says Mark*. We were kind of expecting the critics to pan it, really have a go, but actually they didn't, they were quite complimentary. That was a pleasant surprise and didn't do us any harm, you know.

That was a weird, *weird* year, though, *explains Kian*. It was the first album we'd done without Brian. In a sense, I could see that doing the Rat Pack thing sort of bought us a little time, but it was a sideways step really. I wasn't a massive fan of the project, if I'm being honest. The studio was fun, as the lads have said, but it was all *too old*. People already thought we were older than we were, so that didn't help.

We were doing photo shoots in these beautifully tailored suits. We spent hours being individually measured up with chalk and then remeasured. The stylists they put on that job worked really hard, too – our hair was perfect, we were beautifully groomed, a real eye for detail, it was all done immaculately.

Then we flew to LA and recorded three videos in three days, which we'd never done before either. At first, it was great fun, because it was so different from what we were used to. We were quite natural at it, too. Part of me felt a bit we'd been taken back to our pre-Westlife days, back performing *Grease* or those other Sligo musicals. It was an act, if you like. We stuck to the characters and initially that was brilliant.

Kevin Spacey had made a film playing the part of Bobby Darin and we got to perform with him in London at the launch of the movie. That was cool, too. For me personally, the best part of that project was when our dads formed a band called Dadlife and sang 'That's Life' on our ITV special. It was brilliant!

But that enthusiasm died very fast for all of us. By the time we got to the Christmas promotion, I was thinking, *Thank God we haven't got to sing Rat Pack songs again* ... I'm just being honest with you, here.

The music was classic, for sure, but we felt too *old*. We looked stylish, but in an older man's kinda way. We were only in our mid-twenties ...

It felt like we were in the West End for a year, *agrees Shane*. It actually felt as though we'd got a role in a musical. Those are great songs for party pieces, though, to be fair. If you're ever having a few pints with your mates then you can get up and know all the words to those Rat Pack tunes, so that's one good thing that came out of it!

The tour following *Allow Us to Be Frank* was a bit tricky, *continues Kian*. By this point, we didn't want to be singing Rat Pack songs all night, so instead of doing that we changed the name of the dates to 'The Red Carpet Tour', but then we were worried the fans would hear that and expect just Rat Pack. So we changed the name again, this time to 'The Number Ones Tour' and we sang a segment of Rat Pack mixed in with a lot of our hits.

Westlife had become such a commercial success, *says Nicky* that an album that shifted less than a million copies in the UK was seen as a disappointment. *Allow Us to be Frank* was our worst seller so far, so we were concerned. Plus, as Kian has said, the tour to promote it was fun at first but wasn't the most enjoyable one we'd done.

When we'd finished the Number Ones tour, we took about three months off, which was an unusually long time for us. I'm not sure about the rest of the boys, but I was certainly considering my future. Collectively, we held our hands up and said, 'We need better songs.' So, we called a meeting with Louis because we were all concerned and said, 'We're stale, the media aren't interested in us, we feel the fans are a bit bored of it, the record company is always on about other new bands around us …'

At the beginning of our career, we were the hottest property and we were pushed, pushed, pushed. Every marketing man in every territory got the phone call from the big boss saying, 'Westlife is the priority. You break this album.' Then, after a while, we felt like we'd become just part of the furniture.

People in boxing always say that the last person to know when to retire is the boxer himself; the truth is really that the *first* person to know is the boxer, but he doesn't admit it to himself. At this point I was having doubts. None of us wanted to let it go, we all wanted to do our best to save it, but was it saveable? So, as I've said, I started considering my future. I really thought this was the end of the band. I did an acting course in New York at the New York film academy. I thought if I needed to find a new path, then acting could be it, I'm a very driven person and I was quite happy to start off at the bottom of the ladder again.

*   *   *

A big part of the problem for the *Allow Us to be Frank* tour, *ponders Mark,* was the way it made us look older, as Kian has pointed out. We were already seen as a band who wore suits all the time, and now we were wearing even more of them. In the past, it's often stopped people seeing us as we really are.

Sometimes, for instance, you're walking down the street and people say they are surprised to see you wearing a tracksuit! That's how much the four-men-in-suits image has been driven home. That's a little odd for us because we wear very casual stuff away from the band all the time. We were always pushed as the boys you wouldn't mind your daughter coming home with, and the suits fitted that. But that's only a very small part of what we are and what we do.

Tied in to this is a perception in some quarters that we aren't that interesting. We know that Westlife is treated by some people as open season for slagging off pop. We seem to have become the poster boys for criticizing pop music, a reason to not like it. That doesn't really bother us in the main, but if someone I like disses Westlife, it really hurts me. It's happened a million times.

Take for example, Kate Nash. I heard her debut single and really liked it. I bought the album and thought it was great. I saw her sing on *Later with Jools Holland* and really enjoyed it. I thought she was really good and I told people, I said, 'This is a great album, you should check it out.' Then I heard her in the press saying how she and other women like Amy Winehouse were doing it for the girls and then saying words to the effect of *instead of all that shite like West-life*. I was really hurt by that, even though I don't know her personally. But she doesn't know me personally either. I had to throw her CD in the bin, I couldn't listen to it anymore.

Mind you, I have to be honest, I do like to swap from singer to fan, though with complete double standards! I used to go on, say, *CD: UK* and feel awkward and sing my best but not really feel good about it. I used to think that the lights and the cameras and all that made it so much more complicated than the public realized and how it was a shame that people couldn't be more sympathetic to a bad performance. But then I'd come home late at night from a club and watch a repeat of the same show and see another act on there singing badly and say, 'That was a fucking disgrace!' Naughty, really!

We've been to a million TV studios over the years and there are still certain bands who won't even look at us or acknowledge they know us, just because we are Westlife and to them we are the epitome of what they want to remove themselves from, so they want to make a statement that they are nothing like us.

Sometimes I think it's an accessory for a rock band these days to hate Westlife with a passion, just as much as it is to have black eyeliner or tattoos or whatever. I don't really care, but it's true though. It seems important that you diss Westlife at any given opportunity! Sometimes I can't understand where the passion comes from, the sheer aggression when people comment on Westlife.

It tends to be crap bands who do it. By contrast, the biggest Irish band of the lot, U2, has never said a bad word about us *ever*. They'll have been asked about us a thousand times – the Irish thing, the boy band thing, all that – but not once have I heard them say a bad word about Westlife. And they are what you might call proper celebrities!

If the biggest rock band in the world actually says, 'Fair play to Westlife,' then it kind of puts the sneers of a few fucking smelly little scroats into perspective. Who knows, perhaps in alternative circles where people strive to be different, it will become so commonplace to hate Westlife that suddenly it'll be the coolest thing to actually *love* Westlife.

Maybe!

Not.

Also, I always think no matter how good or successful you are, someone won't be impressed. Even with someone like Prince, who I absolutely idolize – I think he is one of the biggest musical geniuses who has ever walked the face of the Earth – there are a lot of people who think he's an annoying little shit.

Plus, at the end of the day, our fans don't care what the Arctic Monkeys or U2 think of Westlife. They just think what they personally want to about us. If our fans like our music, then they have every right to enjoy it without criticism. If it makes them happy, then that makes us relevant. I'm not trying to change the world or do anything political, I'm literally just singing and some people – quite a few, to be fair – like it. So it's between us and our fans. They like us and we like to perform for them, so why do people feel the need to get in between that relationship? They should just leave us alone and let us and our fans get on with it.

We're having a great time.

*   *   *

People might not see us as the quiet, retiring four men in suits, *says Nicky*, if they were sat in one of our band meetings! There are so many decisions and plans to make in Westlife – it is, after all, a very big business – and, boy, do we have arguments! Things can get very heated. *Very* heated. We've all gone head to head at some point, more so in the early years. To be fair with you, no one has ever struck somebody else. There's been a few kicks and a few little head to heads. I think there was a head butt along the way, one time in America, me and Kian actually. It was more a case of pushing foreheads against one another than an actual butt.

What actually happened, *recalls Kian*, I think I'm right in saying, is this: we'd been working really hard for weeks on end on that American promo jaunt we told you about and we were all really tired. Nicky and me were rowing over something as we walked down the slipway onto a plane. I snapped and said, 'I'll fucking kill you!' and he said, 'No, *I'll* fucking kill *you*!' and we squared up to each other, foreheads touching. We didn't butt each other, it was more of a tiny nudge!

We roared at each other 'You fucking hit me! No one hits a member of the band!'

'I *didn't* fucking hit you! If I *did* fucking hit you, you'd fucking know about it!'

We shouted at each other a little while longer, but it was all over almost before it had started.

We all used to row a lot in the early days and it was almost always over something completely trivial. I laugh out loud now when I think of what we argued over.

We were landing in Asia once and Mark and Shane were sitting across from each other and they were both coming off the back of a 12-hour flight, tired, scraggy and jetlagged, and were really bickering. They were sitting in Business Class with seats facing each other and all of a sudden their feet went up in the air and they started kicking each other like they were on some out-of-control bicycles. We all jumped in and calmed it down. It was hilarious.

Another time, at a photo shoot in Spain, Nicky and Shane were arguing over something and Nicky was wearing a very stylish but very pointy pair of shoes and he just cracked the point of his toe right into Shane's shin. Classic.

Looking back on all those arguments, they were fucking hilarious. I don't even remember what they were about. It was a very surreal environment we lived in and the tiniest issues and tensions could be blown up into giant proportions. We were very young, we'd been around each other every minute of every day for several years, we were touring the world with massive success and fame, often jetlagged, nearly always exhausted – it was a melting pot really. When me and Nicky went head to head, it was probably over who was sitting where or perhaps who did the front cover of which magazine next – just kids' stuff usually. Mickey Mouse bullshit.

We have some *raging* arguments. Sometimes, in the middle of a big row, you wonder if it is a good way of working, but actually it's a *brilliant* way to operate a band. We have four very definite opinions and four very different personalities. And those four people have to be heard. We have a very open and honest band dynamic and, although that can see some pretty big blow-ups, it's the reason why we are still here.

I agree 100 per cent, *says Nicky*. I truly believe those things have to happen to keep the band alive. Opinions are like arseholes, everyone has got one and they all stink. So these discussions are important.

Sometimes, it kicks off big time. I always try, to the best of my ability, to hear everybody's side, but if I'm passionate enough about something, I won't be easily swayed. Kian's the same, he will not be swayed, and that can cause a bit of a clash sometimes. You can end up walking out of the discussions. We never fall out, but we most certainly disagree. Westlife wouldn't work any other way, I believe.

To your average person watching Westlife on telly, I'm able to laugh at the fact that people think we're a boring bunch of twats in black suits with no passion for what we do. Nothing could be further from the truth.

Nicky's right, *says Kian*. We often clash. He has very strong opinions and I am the same, and when you get two characters like that, it can blow up in smoke. I actually think the pair of us handle it very well – we get the decisions made and move on. It's very constructive the way he talks to me and, I think, vice versa. And, I've got to say, we argue over Westlife, we don't argue over anything else. We argue over what's right and what's wrong for the band.

It does get heated, *agrees Shane*, and these meetings can go on for hours sometimes, but we need to do that. People reading this book will now realize that the four members of Westlife don't just get up on stage and sing some songs. We are involved in every element of the band. It's like an empire really. If you think about the band as a business, there are literally hundreds of people involved: the record company, tour staff, management, lawyers, accountants, merchandise people, producers, songwriters, it's almost endless. If we get asked one question by each part of that business, then we might have five or ten major decisions to make every day, things you can't take lightly. We run the band as a democracy, so making those decisions takes time. That dynamic is what makes Westlife tick, it really is. We want to be in control and that brings these debates, it makes our world go round.

To be fair, Kian took on the role of speaking with Louis, they love to gossip, they get on really well and began taking those phone calls then telling us the craic. That brings him a lot of stress, but he enjoys that, he really likes that role. He deals with the record company, too, most of the time. He does it very well and it's great that he took that role on too. He's brilliant at it. Sometimes I think the band wouldn't be together if it weren't for Kian. Me and Mark are seen as lead singers, but Kian's role is vital. And as for Nicky, well, he is so *passionate* about the band that he really wants it to get it right and make the right decisions, he will always want to make sure the band is making the right move and that is amazing too, it drives us to focus and get it right ...

I absolutely hate the politics side of it, *says Nicky* ...

It is a unique chemistry *continues Shane*, and I don't think any other person in the world could fit in. No other singer, no matter how brilliant, could join Westlife. It just wouldn't work.

And ultimately, *says Kian*, as Shane says, we run the band democratically. We started that right back when Louis said he didn't want to work with a boy band with six members, when we sat down at that table and all agreed to take the chance that one of us would get cut. That's how Westlife works and it's very effective ...

And if all else fails, *says Nicky*, we've always got scissors, paper, rock ...

why I got into
this in the first
place...
...To sing!

MARK

CHAPTER NINETEEN

The Human Instinct to Find Love

I'm the type of person who has to be myself to be truly happy, *says Mark*. For a long time, in both Westlife and my private life, I couldn't do that because the general public didn't know that I was gay. So there was a period in my life underlined by darkness and unhappiness.

Let me clarify myself. I wasn't consumed by this issue all day, every day. For starters, I didn't have the time to dwell on it, because being in Westlife is scheduled insanity most days of the year. When you're in a band operating at this level, there are literally weeks that go by when you haven't a moment's peace to think about things. *People even wake you up* – you don't even have to do that for yourself at times. Then it's down to breakfast, after which the schedule for the day is held up and read out by the tour manager, then it's straight into interviews, meetings, studios, travel, flights, show time, then your head hits the pillow, there's a knock on the door and it's the next morning and off you go again.

You hear a lot of celebrities complain about that, but for me personally, with regards to dealing with my sexuality, it was a blessing. It meant that during the period when I wasn't ready to confront my feelings and I wasn't ready to come out publicly, I didn't need to think about it – or rather, I didn't have time to. Westlife was a perfect distraction. The minute you step on stage or do an interview, you go into a mode that basically makes you forget about everything else. It's a shut-off valve from reality. It's almost like you put on the infamous Westlife suit and it's all consuming. I didn't consciously push the issue to the back of my mind, but being in a successful pop band certainly enabled me to do so, intentionally or not, for some time.

I used to half-think to myself, *Yeah, yeah, I'll deal with this, just not yet.*

If there was ever a quiet minute alone, though, I'd sit down and there was definitely a sadness within me.

But I have to stress that I wasn't pretending. I just hadn't come to a conclusion about it yet, there was still a dialogue in my mind that was unresolved.

Then I met Kevin and everything changed.

He'd been in bands himself – he was still in a band called V when I first met him – so he completely understood my way of life in Westlife. He had come out very early on in his life and I admired the pride and courage he possessed; I loved that in him. We got on brilliantly and I loved being with him. Meeting Kevin has been so good for me because not only did I have a boyfriend, someone to have a relationship with, but I'd also met my new best friend. He was someone to share my life with. We had so much to tell, so much to show each other, so much to do, you know.

There was, however, a six-month window when we kept our relationship quiet, but I hated it. Sneaking around, being evasive, it was dreadful. For example, there was a time when Kevin came to see me on tour in Manchester and everyone was going to a club afterwards to have a few drinks and party. We wanted to go but didn't, because I knew that without a doubt everyone was going to put two and two together if we did and initially I wasn't yet ready for that.

But very quickly, my growing feelings for Kevin became the catalyst for me to come out. I had fallen in love with someone I wanted to share everything with, learn from, be around, just be my other half, and yet I was 'supposed' to not tell anyone.

I was in heaven but only in secret.

Well, I wasn't having it!

I began to think, *You know what? I'm loving this and I'm so happy right now. Everything I'm doing is good, nothing here needs hiding or covering up. All I'm doing is enjoying myself with my other half, my boyfriend.*

Before I knew it, I wanted to come out in public.

I always think that you can't really complain about things unless you have made some effort to change them. Even if that effort comes to nothing, at least you've tried. Sexuality is such a massive part of anyone's personality, it's in their blood, so it has to be expressed, otherwise there is a big hole right in the middle of that person, a constant emptiness. I knew that in order for me to be 100 per cent happy, I had to come out. There had to be a change. I had the money, the cars, the nice house and lots of material things, but the core of my life needed more. I finally realized that my ultimate happiness would involve dealing with my sexuality. I'd put it off long enough.

The day came and I was very, very happy. Bring it on! You might think of a gay pop star sitting in his house, crying at the thought of coming out and all the fall-out – nothing could be further from the truth. I knew it was going to be in all the papers the next day and I welcomed that. That's how ready I was.

It was *exciting*.

Forget about all the pop-star headlines, the music business, the papers, the celebrity, all of the peripheral stuff – the reason I was ready to tell the world I was gay was because of the simple human instinct to find love and be attracted to someone. I yearned to have someone close, to share things with, to live my life with. That impenetrable shell I'd put up around me – against coming out, against the music business, against anything that might steal me away from my beautiful life back in Ireland – had been rock solid, but Kevin dismantled it in seconds, to be honest. I'd packed it all up so tightly inside me that once it started to unravel, it just fell open within minutes.

As soon as it was public knowledge I was gay, *everything* felt completely natural and absolutely right. It was the start of the rest of my life and I was ecstatic.

And do you know what?

The boys were ecstatic for me too.

And so was Louis.

And, fantastically, so were the fans.

I'd come out to the boys some time previously and they'd never been anything other than completely supportive, brilliant. The thing is, we spend so much time together and they just wanted me to be happy. Kevin made me happy, so for them that was all that mattered. They genuinely did not care if it impacted on the band at all, as long as I was happy. They knew how much it meant to me to be with someone, so they couldn't wait to meet Kevin, and when they did, they loved him and got on like a house on fire.

As you know, Louis had spoken with Shane and Nicky about their girlfriends in the early days, so you might think he'd have been more reserved. Do you know what he said to me when I told him I was going to come out to the fans?

'Brilliant! Mark, I'm so pleased for you!'

Louis was very supportive. Not for a second did he think or care about how it would affect the band's image, its record sales, nothing. He was great. I can still hear him now, saying, 'This is great, Mark! Great!'

I can honestly say I had *not one* bad remark or letter. Not one. Things really have changed so much for the better in society.

One thing I will say about the whole experience is how crucial the support of your friends and family is. My parents, grandparents, family and friends went out of their way to make sure I knew just how much they loved me and how proud of me they were, telling me I was no different to them than the day before. This can be long before someone comes out, it might be unnoticed by others, say perhaps a comment about a TV show, or about a gay celebrity in a magazine, by the way they generally react and comment about things. You might think certain people won't like it, when in fact they will be very supportive. Don't assume the worst. Once you come out and make that step, you will find there are loads of people around that support you and love you and that you'll never be alone. Good people build up this reserve of confidence in you that means when the time comes, everything will be okay. In fact, it will be better than okay, it will be *fantastic*.

Now that it is all behind me and no longer an issue on any level, I feel so strongly for people who are still trapped behind this obstacle – people who don't have the support they deserve, people who aren't confident enough to come out. The thought of never coming out, as some people sadly do, and living to a ripe old age behind a mask, is just too awful. When I hear of people getting very messed up or, worse still, harming themselves over it, I'm horrified.

I'm very aware that opinions and public perceptions of gay men and women have improved dramatically, but things have to keep changing to make the situation as easy as possible for people. There are still such technical words used to skirt around the subject. I don't call Kevin my partner, for instance, like so many people do. He's my *boyfriend*. If you are a straight man, you introduce someone to your girlfriend. Why should a gay man be any different? Why say my 'partner'? Last time I checked, I don't run a business with him. Hopefully, things will change in time and I just look forward to a day when it is the same for everyone. If someone gets to come out, no matter at what age, then it has to be a good thing. You can't be suffocated like that, it's too sad.

As a result of being a gay man who is also known in the public eye, I've been called a role model for coming out and living my life openly and proudly. That's very flattering, but I am rather uncomfortable with that tag. It feels very serious. What I will say is that if I could help someone in a similar situation to mine, give them strength, perhaps a few ideas or even a little bit of confidence to come out and make their life happier, then that would mean the world to me, it really would. More than any number 1, any sell-out tour, it is very special to have that positive effect on someone else's life.

One particular occasion stands out, specifically the first time this happened. People often say, 'I played this Westlife song at my wedding,' stuff like that, and it's great, I love hearing about that impact on people's lives. But nothing like that has hit me as hard and as deeply as one night, about a year after I came out, when a young lad came up to me in a Sligo nightclub and told me how my coming out had helped him. Being a young Irish man, his youth would have been quite similar to mine in terms of his sexuality – I had never seen two guys walking up the street hand in hand for example; homosexuality was not something that was publicly displayed. This young guy said that his mum had the paper with an article about me and he mentioned it to her and then seized the moment to come out to his parents. He said it was all brilliant afterwards and that he just wanted to thank me personally for helping that happen.

I was choked, but I didn't want him to see me that emotional, so I politely thanked him and had a little chat. He said he was a fan and I was a bit like, *If I let on to him how much this means to me ...* There were definite tears in my eyes and I was stuttering, but I stayed composed and didn't really let on, so we chatted some more, then went our separate ways.

After he'd gone, I couldn't stop thinking about his story and what had happened, it had a huge impact on me. I sat at home later going over what he'd said. If someone comes up and says, 'I loved your last album,' I'm like, 'Oh, cool, thanks!' If they say, 'I loved your vocal on this song,' it does make me smile and changes my mood. But when something like that happens, it literally makes me want to cry with joy – however soft I might sound saying that, it genuinely brings me joy. It's happened on a few occasions since, but even if that had been the only time, it is something I will take with me when I leave this planet as one of my proudest moments in life.

When you have an encounter like with that lad in the Sligo night-club, it gives you the sharpest perspective in a second.

I've been lucky enough to come out and be delighted with the consequences. I wish I had done so a long time before, because it really wasn't as big a deal as I had built it up to be. People reacted brilliantly to me and my life has changed infinitely for the better since. Since I broke those walls down, I've enjoyed things so much more and something has lit up inside me. Now I can embrace life knowing what is important to me and I am very grateful for that.

*　　*　　*

We had our own thoughts, so it wasn't a big surprise, *said Shane*. We were just so relieved he was able to tell us, we were made up for him. We were all just over the moon and we gave him a hug, we were so excited. You could see he was so relieved at our reaction, but how else would we react?

He was comfortable straight away. It was a great day for him and for us. It takes an awful lot of balls to do what Mark did normally, but because he is famous and he knew there would be attention on him, it must have been extra hard. It must have taken an awful lot of guts. Since then he has become someone that a lot of people look up to, and rightly so. Young guys look up to him and I'm proud of him for his courage and for being himself.

I wasn't surprised at all, *added Kian*, you could sense it had been coming, he just needed time to get his own thoughts together. I just said, 'Great!' I was delighted for him and you could see a burden had been lifted straight away.

Although it was such a huge deal for him at the time, now we don't even think about it. Mark is Mark, and he has Kevin, and that's the way it is. I love the fact that now he doesn't need to worry about that ever again.

When Mark told us he was gay, *recalls Nicky*, I was delighted for him. I had tears in my eyes. It seemed such a relief, I could see a weight had lifted off him and there was an element of that for the band as well. We were all just *so* pleased. Mark is the deepest thinker of the band, so we knew how much it would have meant to him and how much he would have been thinking it all through. Once he'd come to terms with things in his own head and then shared it with his loved ones, he was a much happier man.

At the time, if it had altered the band at all, if there had been any negative repercussions whatsoever, we just felt, so be it. Even if it meant the end of the band, so be it, Mark had to be happy. We didn't think our fans were that fickle, we knew them better than that, but if Mark coming out had caused us any problems at all, we wouldn't have cared – it was far, far more important for him to be happy. Some things in life are much bigger than any band could ever be. As it turned out, as Mark's explained, he didn't get one single negative comment or letter.

There was a big change in Mark immediately afterwards. He was able to walk down the street with Kevin, hold hands, kiss in public, have dinner, go to clubs or events together, just be a couple. He is entitled to that and so is Kevin. He'd not had his life as he wanted it for some time and then suddenly it all changed and I think he couldn't believe how much better it all was, how much easier it became for them both. He's become more outgoing too, he's got new friends, a new confidence – it's been brilliant. We are so close as people and we knew this was as big a subject as anything for him, like us having children. We were – and are – very conscious of keeping it private, though – it really is his private life.

In 2006 Mark took the band to a gay club together in Dublin. All four of us went and it was *pandemonium*. We are pretty well-known faces in Dublin anyway – individually you get stopped a lot and asked to have your picture taken, to sign autographs, all that, pretty constantly – but for all four of us to go out together, to a gay club, it was mayhem!

When we got there, it was karaoke night as well, so we had the best time. It was brilliant, too, because we were with Mark and I felt like the great night was a celebration *for* Mark.

Since then, he's been able to completely relax. Everyone knows now and he is much, much happier.

Without a doubt, it is one of the happiest moments in the band, as far as I am concerned.

THE NOISE THE LAUGHS
THE SMILES THAT I SEE
FROM STAGE AS HE SING
AND DANCE AROUND
HAVE BEEN PERMANENTLY
IMPRINTED AS LIFELONG
MEMORIES FOR ME

Nicky

CHAPTER TWENTY

'A MADCAP STROKE OF GENIUS'

With Brian gone and the Rat Pack album finished, *remembers Shane*, we all felt like we really had a point to prove with the next album, our seventh. There was definitely the feeling in the band that if this next album wasn't massive, it could all be coming to an end. We didn't want to be a band that sold 700,000 copies of an album in the UK – not that there's anything wrong with that – but we were used to, and still wanted, to sell a million plus every year. We had a point to prove. We had to make the first original pop album since Brian left. We needed a new lease of life. We knew that. The record company knew that. There were even whispers that some bands get dropped ...

We had to put out a big album to keep Westlife at the top level.

And any big album needed to have big singles.

For several months, Louis had been telling us about a song he wanted us to record. Simon wasn't into it at first, but Louis was insistent, he was certain it would be big. It was a tune that had been knocking around for a couple of years.

That song was called, 'You Raise Me Up' and, for Westlife, it changed *everything*.

The song was written by Brendan Graham and Rolf Loveland, an Irishman and a Norwegian guy. Brian Kennedy had recorded it in Ireland and Josh Groban had released it in the States and then sold millions of albums because of it, so it was not a new song, it had been out already in various forms and in numerous genres – in fact, it had been recorded in 125 languages!

So, to be honest, when Louis said, 'Why don't you try this?' I actually said, 'Louis, you're fucking mad.'

I did.

I thought it was one of his madcap schemes.

It was.

A madcap stroke of genius.

We didn't see it like that at first, *admits Mark*. After the Rat Pack album, it was so nice to be listening to demos of pop music again. We are pop singers and we are proud of that fact, so it was a relief to get back to that. We had a meeting and they played us this demo of 'You Raise Me Up'. If I remember rightly, the demo was actually pretty ordinary. I think some of the band thought it was a joke. I really liked it, but I did worry how commercial it was, if I am being honest.

At the same time, it was something Louis thought would work and when he says that, you *have* to listen to his reasons. Louis has been in the music industry for years. He knows his stuff. He isn't just a marketing person, he's a marketing *genius*, I truly believe that. But he's not a marketing *nerd*. He doesn't make decision based on facts and figures and studies and statistics. He just brainstorms and comes out with these big, mad ideas and three out of four – sometimes four out of four – will be incredible.

When I first heard 'You Raise Me Up', *says Nicky*, I thought it sounded like something you'd sing in church. I liked it, but I didn't think it was a single. I couldn't hear it on radio, I couldn't see it being used on TV ...

... and there was another song in the picture for the single, a song called 'Amazing', a mid-tempo song, *recalls Shane*. For a while the band was pushing for 'Amazing' as a single.

The first time I actually heard 'You Raise Me Up', *says Kian*, was when I went to Simon Cowell's home in LA for lunch with Jodi. We were chatting about everything – Westlife, the music industry in general, all sorts. Then he asked me if I knew the song. I said yes, and he asked if I thought it would be good for Westlife. I said it was a great song, but wasn't it already well known? But I also said it was worth a try, why not?

As a band, however, we were quite adamant that we would go with 'Amazing'. It was up tempo and *young*. We felt it was like 'I Want It That Way' by the Backstreet Boys, and the record company loved it too.

In hindsight, Simon Cowell made the right choice, though, because the sound of songs like 'Amazing' wasn't doing as well as it used to. Plus it wasn't typical Westlife. Simon wanted a crossover song. So, yes, Louis mentioned the idea first, then Simon reinforced it, drove it home.

Then I took a call from Sonny, who said, 'Well, will you first listen to the most recent arrangement of 'You Raise Me Up' please? I think you'll change your mind ...'' We'd heard about six different arrangements by this point, but this final one was brilliant. We had a listen and decided as a band to go with 'You Raise Me Up' after all.

There are lots of versions of 'You Raise Me Up' out there, *points out Mark*. We could see the appeal, so when we got into the studio, we started to sing it and play around with ideas. I was singing with Shane, swapping lines, experimenting, and it suddenly started to sound like a *massive* Westlife song. I heard a nice gospel element in it and I sang it with that in mind. I really enjoyed recording with the gospel choir. What hadn't made much sense on the demo worked perfectly when me and Shane recorded it. The song just seemed to suit our voices. By the time it was finished, we had this perfect Westlife record, almost out of the blue.

We'd all recorded our parts for the song separately, *explains Shane*, so we were unaware what the final mix sounded like before we all sat round that table listening to the playback. The hairs stood up on my neck, it was one of those moments, we were looking around at each other, stunned, thinking, *Christ, this song is massive. This is unreal.*

Even then, though, *recalls Shane*, I wasn't sure if it should be the lead single. This was the track that would effectively launch the second phase of our career, the time after Brian had left. But we'd already got some opinions; we'd played the track to our families, our friends back home. The reaction was incredible – they all loved it and said we should go for it.

The atmospheric black-and-white video for the single was superb. The director hit the nail on the head; in fact the record company nailed it in every way.

'You Raise Me Up' was released in November 2005.

It went straight in at number 1.

It won Record of the Year.

Our corresponding album, *Face to Face*, was massive, entering the charts at the top and knocking Robbie Williams off the number 1 slot after only a week.

We were nominated for Best Pop Act at the Brit Awards, the first time we'd been nominated since 2002.

It just kept getting bigger as well. The first public event we did with that song, *recounts Nicky*, was at the Royal Albert Hall for a breast cancer charity. I'd just lost my 32-year-old cousin, Debbie, a month before that to breast cancer, so it was a pretty weird experience for me personally.

When we sang 'You Raise Me Up' live, the audience reaction was unbelievable. Staggering. We knew then that something was happening with that song. You could just feel it. The song had a life of its own.

'You Raise Me Up' took us back round the world again. We went down to Australia and did that song on three TV shows – we were only there for four days – then we left and the album went straight in at number 1 down there. Australia was somewhere we really wanted to break, because apart from America, it was the main territory we just couldn't crack. We had New Zealand, we had all of Asia and Africa, we had Europe. Now we had Australia too.

When we went to Australia with that song, *reminisces Mark*, it was one of the nicest times ever in Westlife. All our other halves came down with us for a start. Also, because that was our first number 1 down there, we were treated like a new band, everything was fresh and people were so enthusiastic and excited. I remember the girl who plays Sally from *Home & Away* coming to the launch party and that was a very strange feeling, because I loved that soap. We were going on all the big TV shows, travelling and meeting loads of new people and we were with our loved ones, partying. It was brilliant.

The song was so international, *says Kian*, it even broke us in mainland China. We'd always done well in Hong Kong, but to break mainland China was amazing, very rare for a Western band …

'You Raise Me Up' was a real blessing for us, *continues Mark*. To me, it was exactly what we needed to be doing. It was a world-class hit on a worldwide level. It's only a personal opinion, but you put something like 'Mandy' next to that song and it just doesn't stand up.

'You Raise Me Up', *says Nicky*, was like a footballer who is nearing the end of his contract scoring the winner in the FA Cup final at Wembley. We only had one album left to run with Sony-BMG and, don't forget, the Rat Pack album had been seen as far from a commercial hit. But now, we had 'You Raise Me Up' behind us and it changed everything. 'You Raise Me Up' was just enormous, our biggest single yet – and all this at a time when downloads were crucifying singles sales.

We negotiated a colossal new record deal in the aftermath of the song's release.

Remember, only a few weeks previously, there had been that moment before the song came out when we thought we might even get dropped.

Suddenly there was no chance of the band coming to an end. It felt like the whole band situation had been re-energized completely.

That song was – and still is – a phenomenon.

I do believe 'You Raise Me Up' took Westlife to the next level, *agrees Kian*. It saved us in a sense, because things could have slipped and disappeared. That song put us back up there. It was a worldwide hit and it made everything feel like the early days again. It gave us a genuine new lease of life. Suddenly everyone was excited about the band again. At the end of the day, we're in the music industry and if the music isn't good enough, you might as well go home.

I think the record company got the corresponding album, *Face to Face*, absolutely spot on, *says Shane*. Even the cover was well thought out. Our four heads together, it fitted with the fans facing our music, the need for us to have a big album – it *just worked*. With the windfall of publicity and acclaim and success that 'You Raise Me Up' gave us, we were off on an absolute flyer and we never looked back.

Without a doubt, 'You Raise Me Up' not only saved our career, but gave it that jump-start we needed to get back to the highest level. It's a massive part of our career and to Brendan Graham and Rolf

Loveland, I say thank you for writing that song.

* * *

We've done several high-profile collaborations, *recalls Nicky*, such as with Mariah and Donna Summer. With Diana Ross, it was very different from Mariah Carey. We were doing the old hit 'When You Tell Me That You Love Me' for a winter 2005 release. As we were getting ready, one of her people came in and said, 'Now, gentlemen, please address her as Miss Ross.' Even the director had to call her that. I don't get that. I'm not one to cause a fuss about it, but I don't really have much conversation about it, to be honest.

Towards the end of the day, we asked if we could have a picture with Miss Ross and she said yes. Then, when our security man got the camera out – just a family snaps type camera – she said, 'Who are these people with cameras?' I explained and she said it was OK but that the picture couldn't be used publicly. So all we have is that one shot of us with her. To be fair, though, she turned up on time at 9 a.m. and worked very hard until late that day. She certainly grafted and put the hours in, that Miss Ross.

* * *

Around this time we were doing a fairly big promo tour in Asia, *recalls Nicky*. For some reason on this trip my stomach was all over the place. I had the shits really bad. I took some tablets, but it was no use, there were regular and severe explosions.

We all met up and piled into the people carrier for a short journey to a TV station. We pulled out on to a main road crammed with traffic hurtling past, only for my stomach to start rumbling again.

'Er, driver, how long will it take to get to the TV station please?'

It was only about ten minutes, but by the time we got there I was desperate. I jumped out of the car before it had even stopped and ran in, past the reception and suffered another Asiatic explosion in the gents just in time.

We were there to do a pre-record of some songs. As they were doing our make-up, I had to go to the loo again. It was ridiculous.

Then we got called out and went up to the studio to start filming.

As I stood next to my mic, my stomach started rumbling again.

I was thinking, *Mind over matter, Nicky, keep calm ...*

Then it really started rumbling ...

After every song, I needed another toilet trip and I'm sure the studio audience were wondering what on Earth I was doing. The TV lights were so hot I was sweating like a pig, I was off-colour, gaunt from being ill – I was a wreck.

Then the music came on for the last song in the set, 'You Raise Me Up'.

We were on top form, singing beautifully, looking immaculate – classic Westlife.

'When I am down, and, oh, my soul so weary ...'

More stomach rumbling, this time really bad.

'When troubles come and my heart burdened be ...'

I was pretty burdened myself by the time we were halfway through the song.

As Shane reached the finale, my stomach went nuclear ...

He went into his solo closing line: 'You raise me up ...'

Gurgle, gurgle, gurgle ...

'To more ...'

Jeez, for Christ's sake, Shane, hurry up ...

'Than I ...'

Oh, for fuck's sake, man, pleeeaassee ...

'Can ...'

We're nearly there, come on, Shane, come on ...

Shane?

He held that last pause for what seemed like an hour ... It was probably the same pause as always, but I was about to have a major personal incident on TV, so I turned to him and said, 'I can't fucking wait any longer to get out of here!' – at which point he burst out laughing and completely fluffed his last note.

The director said, 'Sorry, chaps, that was no good, let's run from the top ...'

'Run' was exactly what I did, in more ways than one.

Seeing all your faces
looking up at us singing
every word of our songs
is truly the best
feeling in the world.

CHAPTER TWENTY-ONE

FAMILY

We were actually on tour in Dublin when my twin baby boys arrived, *recalls Nicky*. Georgina wasn't due for another eight weeks, so it was all a bit worrying. She had some tell-tale signs, so we went to hospital. They kept her in for observation that day and that evening I went off and did the first of the 12 shows at the Point Depot in Dublin. I went back to the hospital after the show, saw her and made sure she was OK, then I went back home to sleep at about 2 a.m.

The phone rang at 6.45 the next morning, I rushed straight over to the hospital and called my mam on the way. I heard later on that Mam and my nana had the candles lit and were praying as they waited on the news. My boys, Rocco and Jay, were born at 9.55 a.m. by emergency C-section. What an experience that was. Georgina said I looked like George Clooney from *ER* – funny. Wow, my heart was pounding. I now had two little boys and they were so small.

I was obviously worried because they were very small – Rocco was just 2lb 13 oz and Jay was 3lb 11 oz – but our professor, Fionnuala McCauliffe, said to me, 'They're fine, they're perfectly healthy. They're very underweight, but they are in the right place and your show must go on!' Amazing.

We caught G's mam Miriam on the hop because she was on holiday in Chile. Somewhere like Spain would have been easier! It took me a couple of hours to get hold of her and give her the news of her grandsons' arrival. She'd only just landed and had to fly straight back home. I also remember the promoter ringing me and congratulating me and then going, 'Are the gigs still on?'

I really want to say this, though – the vibe around Dublin and Ireland for me at the time was just incredible. It seemed as though everyone in the street was stopping me – they obviously knew who Georgina's dad was – and it was in the news, on the radios, people were like 'beep beep' on their car horns. Fair play to everyone. It was like I'd won an election or scored a World Cup winning goal! People were so warm and supportive, I'll never forget that.

Then the crowd at the Point Depot that night … Oh my God, how to describe it! I had tears in my eyes the whole show, it was just like a fairytale. I remember Louis coming up to me going, 'This is like a soap opera, you couldn't write this!' I would do these shows, literally thinking of Georgina and the boys all the time, how they were, then race to the hospital, grab some sandwiches, see them, say goodnight, catch a few hours' sleep, then go back to the hospital all day, then do the next show. It was manic but brilliant. I did those 12 shows on pure adrenaline.

There were paparazzi outside the hospital every morning and every evening; I was getting photographed every day. I was on national radio and Ireland's biggest chat show, *The Late Late Show*, as well as the front pages of every newspaper. It was a crazy time.

Then Georgina was coming home, but the babies had to stay in ICU for a while yet. Footballers get some serious money and pop stars get some serious money, but nurses and doctors – man, they are life-savers! We were obviously very sad that the babies had to stay behind, but we stood on the hospital steps and I said a few words to the media. Georgina couldn't talk. Then we got in the car and drove home and what I'd just said came on the radio.

The house had been a building site when we'd left before, but our interior designer Paschal had performed a miracle at renaissance interiors and it was all ready for the babies. The nursery was beautiful.

It's a most amazing thing, becoming a parent, and the way the babies arrived was surreal, in the middle of a tour! It was a really hard time for me and Georgina, especially Georgina, being in and out of the hospital for feeds every morning, afternoon and evening for five weeks. It took its toll – we were exhausted. We both cried every night at leaving the boys in there without us. It was heartbreaking.

Jay finally arrived home first – Rocco was to come a week later – and I remember sitting in this big house with this tiny baby in the cot, motionless, just listening to him breathing.

Now I've got them both home, I couldn't be happier. Rocco and Jay have changed my life, I am so lucky.

*   *   *

The greatest day of my life, *recalls Shane*, was Saturday 23 July 2005, when my beautiful daughter Nicole was born. Best day ever, for sure, nothing comes close to having your first baby.

We'd obviously been waiting excitedly for our due date, but Gillian had a few problems around 37 weeks into her pregnancy and we were told she'd need to go in for a c-section the very next morning. That was strange, because we'd been looking forward to the baby coming so much, but we weren't sure when; then, all of a sudden, someone was saying, 'The baby will be here tomorrow morning.'

We slept really well, surprisingly, but very early the next morning, I was bouncing around the room, I was wide awake, so excited! I was more awake than I'd ever been in my life! I was bouncing round like a lunatic.

I couldn't wait to be a dad.

Once Gillian had gone into surgery, it was pretty nerve-wracking. I put on a green surgical gown and got to pretend to be a doctor for a short while. They took her in alone at first, to get started and I remember one of the surgeon's assistants came out and, by way of reassuring me, said, 'It's all OK, they've made the first incision!'

Great, thanks. Like I'd feel much better knowing that.

I'm only messing, because the team at Sligo General were fantastic. Dr Carthage and his team were brilliant. It's a major operation. I went in after 'the first incision' and stood by Gillian's head. They'd put this sheet up by her chest to act as a screen from what was happening, but I could see over it and I kept peeping. Then I saw the precise moment that Nicole's head popped out. I'll never forget it, her little head, eyes closed but looking towards me. It was incredible. I just started crying my eyes out and so did Gillian. We were proper bawling, we were so happy. I was so ecstatic.

We had a few names, but as soon as we saw her it was Nicole, without a doubt. She was only just over 5 lbs, quite small, but she was out of hospital after four days and it was brilliant to have her home with us. She slept in the little Moses basket and I learned to sleep with one eye open!

It's an indescribable feeling, becoming a parent, but any father reading this book will know it. You don't know how to deal with it, but it's all happiness, all happiness. Best moment of my life, without a doubt.

*　　*　　*

The tour for *Face to Face* was great, *says Shane*, partly because I *really* loved singing many of the songs night after night. I know that some people often wonder how you stay interested in the same songs for weeks, sometimes months, and when we are up on that stage, I can imagine people wondering if we mean it or if we are going through the motions.

Let me tell you, with Westlife, that's never the case.

Not least because we have certain songs that are just a privilege to sing to people.

The obvious example is 'You Raise Me Up'. Along with 'Flying without Wings', it's our anthem, and I just don't ever get sick of singing it. It's one of those songs, it has this unbelievable effect on me every time I start singing it. I always think about my family when I'm singing that, my mum and dad: 'You raise me up so I can stand on mountains.' Singing those words always makes me proud of what I've done in the band and it's because of my parents that I have done that and I want them to be proud of me. Same with 'Flying without Wings' and the line 'Some find it in the face of their children, some find it in their lover's eyes'. I might be in front of 20,000 people, but at that precise moment, it is the most personal emotion in the world.

I project myself like this every single time. When I'm on stage, I do try and put myself within the song and try and take some meaning out of it. We don't write a lot of our songs, so you have to *feel* the words – I try to imagine if I had written them, what the lyrics would mean, what the creator was thinking when he put those words on paper. As far as I am concerned, if I do this, I sing the songs better. It's a fact.

It works the same way when you record songs too. These top recording studios are so technological, so spotless, so precise, that you have to find a way of taking yourself out of that environment and injecting raw emotion into your voice. Steve Mac is brilliant at helping singers do that. We've worked with him a lot over the years and he's always been an expert at getting emotions out of you. Our Swedish songwriters are brilliant at getting the power of the song and the importance of every note; Steve works on the emotion. Both ways are brilliant.

In the first instance, Steve will ask you to read the lyrics through a few times, then he'll play the song through repeatedly too, telling you to think about the meaning. He'll tell me to think of Nicole, or Gillian. Then, he'll just begin recording, start playing the song and see what comes out when I sing. By this point, I've forgot I'm in a multi-million pound studio, I might as well be singing in me sitting room. I am singing that song to me mum, dad, wife or Nicole right there and then.

Skip forward to 2007, we had a song on the ninth album called 'Already There', which is all to do with being away from your child.

The song was written by Lonestar, who also wrote my all-time favourite track, 'Amazing', which, for me, is my and Gillian's song. I'd been away from home and from Nicole for three agonizing weeks – too long! I go mad in the head after about five or six days, and two weeks is really tough, but three weeks! It was killing me, man. I read the lyrics to 'Already There' and it slaughtered me, 'He called her on the road from a lonely, cold, hotel room, just to hear her say "I love you" ... A little voice came on the phone, said, "Daddy, when you coming home ...?"'

I started crying. I'm not ashamed to admit it, it really upset me. Those words just summed up how I was feeling, I'd been away too long and thinking of her phoning me and talking about her imaginary friend, the sunshine in her hair, Jesus, it cut me up. I have to be really honest and say that I was actually crying in the recording booth and some of those words sung through my tears are on the recorded version of that song. I was crying on every take, I was honestly crying for an hour solid, I couldn't help it. It's the first and only time I have recorded a song while crying, but the feelings were just so raw. You couldn't get any more emotional in the studio.

Nicky pushed so much for us to record the song. He'd got his twins by then and he absolutely loved it ...

Never before had I been touched so vividly and emotionally by a song, *says Nicky*. We were in Sweden recording and the producers played it to me. Rocco and Jay were about three months old and BANG, it hit me like a right hook. I was in ribbons. I recorded it while crying my eyes out, and played it to G., then played it to the lads. They initially weren't too keen on another cover, but I said, 'Wait till you hear the lyrics. And I quickly convinced Shane. It is my favourite from the album and, for me, it should have been the first single instead of 'Home' ...

Nicky was telling me about it, *said* Shane, then I read those lyrics and it was all over, oh, my good God. I was literally sobbing in the booth and I didn't care because I was singing it so well and getting the emotion out.

What a song.

I'm so happy on stage, it's unbelievable, like. When I'm on stage, bar literally having Nicole with me and holding her and hugging her and Gillian, it's probably the happiest time, to be there. So every time I sing that song on stage, I think of recording it and I think of Nicole and I think of those words that say so much. Even if she's at home in bed in Sligo and I'm on stage in Stockholm, in my head I'm singing to her, and for those few minutes, it's all alright, like.

Who knows where I
am or what I'm doing
as you read this, but
whatever the case, know
that I'm very proud
and happy to have
you as a fan, you
mean the world to me!

MARK

MARK xx   *(signature)*   Shane   Nicky

CHAPTER TWENTY-TWO

GOOD DISTRACTIONS

'Nicky, it's Louis. How you doing?'

I was on holiday in Crete, sitting watching the World Cup, when he phoned.

'Hey, Louis, what's happening?'

'Cowell wants to do a love songs cover album, so pick your favourite 25 songs or so, send them through to me and we'll talk some more when you get back.'

Well that's ok, that's a covers album and not what I'd expected. I'm not sure how the rest of the lads will feel about it but I could see it could work. Still, Louis and Simon know what they are doing, so I went with it! Seriously, though, I didn't mind choosing the songs, that was quite fun.

I was walking round the garden holding Nicole, who was just a baby, *said Shane*, when my mobile rang. It was Louis.

I have to admit I wasn't overly keen on a themed album, to be perfectly honest, but with Simon and Louis you have to listen to what their idea is, they've had so much success and deserve your respect. We'd been scouting round for great original songs for a while and we weren't happy with what we were finding, so the 'love album' concept was a good one, it made sense. We didn't want to take a year off at that stage.

The project wasn't without its hitches, however, *remembers Nicky*. We were flying in to sing Bonnie Tyler's 'Total Eclipse of the Heart' on the BBC Lottery show, a song which was lined up to be our next single. It wasn't in London, it was in some tiny studio in the middle of nowhere which hadn't got the facilities to sing live, so we had to mime.

We had to get a helicopter there and it was a freezing cold night. I was sitting in this chopper with our tour manager, security guy and Shane. I strapped myself in and when I looked up, the windscreen and windows were all completely frosted over, you couldn't see out at all. As we'd walked towards the helicopter, I'd noticed it had landed in the middle of some really tall trees.

'Do you reckon he'll be able to sort these windows out, Shane?'

'Yeah, course, not a problem, Nicky,' he replied.

The pilot climbed in and was getting ready to take off. We were all watching him a little nervously, even Shane, and he's got a helicopter so he knows what he's talking about. We were literally waiting for the demister to kick in any second and clear the windscreen.

Then the pilot flips open his window panel, grabs the cuff of his jacket in his palm, leans out of the helicopter and scrubs a small bit of frost off the windscreen, about the size of a dinner plate.

I looked back at Shane and just raised an eyebrow.

Then the pilot started up the rotor blades ...

Here I was, sitting in a freezing cold helicopter, windscreen iced over, on my way to mime to a Bonnie Tyler song.

Actually, although it all sounds very comical now, at the time it was a real shot across the bows for me. I'd left Georgina back home and we'd recently found out she was pregnant. People do die in helicopters and private planes. It happens.

The day after we sang on the Lottery show, I got a call from Louis. He said Simon wanted to pull 'Total Eclipse' as the single. He said he'd thought we looked bored off our tits and, do you know what? He'd hit the nail on the head. We'd been standing there in the suits, miming, 'Turn around, every now and then ...' and I've got to be honest, I was thinking, *For fuck's sake, we're better than this.*

Once again, though, with regard to the album idea, Simon was right, *points out Shane. The Love Album* was massive, selling a million copies in the UK alone. We have always, as a band, gauged our success on how many copies of an album we sell in the UK. We might be doing three or four million around the world, and that's important, but it's also hard to put in context, so we always look to UK sales. This might sound ridiculous, but we look to the million copies mark for every record. That's a lot of albums. I know many bands don't come anywhere near that mark and are very happy. Fair play like, but we're victims of our own success, I guess!

The money is nice, of course, but it's the success that drives us. If the label said, 'Here's twice as much money as you'd normally get, but we think this album will only sell half as many,' I wouldn't take it. We do try to be perfectionists and I'm not ashamed of saying that at all. It's the way I am. You are used to what you are used to, and we always want to work an album hard and sell a million.

* * *

I first met Jodi Albert, *says Kian*, when I was 19 at Party in the Park in London. Our record label had a marquee in the backstage area for their acts and guests and I was chatting to Simon Cowell when Jodi walked out of it. She was so beautiful. I looked at her then turned to Simon and said, 'Oh my God, who is that?' and he replied, 'No, no, no, kiddo, she's not for you.' He explained that Jodi was only 15 at that point. He then introduced us and we chatted when we saw each other throughout the rest of the day. She was signed to Simon's label with the band Girl Thing, who he hoped would be the next Spice Girls. We got on very well straight away, even though I was just over three years older. There was definitely a connection – she was such a beautiful girl, so bubbly and loads of fun. At the after-show party, she was there and we were chatting and messing about, flirting quite a bit.

For the next year, we would bump into each other an awful lot on the circuit. Girl Thing and Westlife were both very busy, so we'd see each other at TV studios, photo sessions, record company offices, and so on. One time, both bands were in Italy performing. We had a great time and chatted loads again. Brian was actually dating a girl out of Jodi's band, so we saw them socially quite a bit too. One time we went to the cinema with Nicky and Brian and I sat next to Jodi. We were flirting again, throwing popcorn at each other, that kind of stuff. For that first year, there was a lot of flirting.

Sadly, Girl Thing didn't work out. It started off well but then sort of imploded. Jodi went off and I didn't see her for about a year. She got really into dancing – she is one of these multi-talented people who can do most things – so she became a professional dancer.

One time my phone rang and it was Louis Walsh saying, 'Kian, you'll never guess who I'm on a video shoot with?' Jodi was the lead dancer for the promotional campaign for a young artist called Omreo Mumba and Louis was with her. He put her on the phone and we chatted for ages.

It seemed that no matter what was happening in either of our careers, she was always a very big part of my life. We were phoning each other even if we weren't seeing each other and we'd chat for hours. I'd sometimes phone her at three in the morning, drunk, and she'd laugh at me! Then she got a part in *Hollyoaks* and that really took off for her. I'd be seeing her in magazines and newspapers the whole time. Even then, deep down, I knew I would end up with this woman, it was just a matter of timing.

That year, before Christmas, I phoned her again and we started being in contact a wee bit more. I said, 'Next time you're in London, why don't we go for a coffee?' Now at this point, she was pretty much 'the *Hollyoaks* girl'; she was in all the magazines, she was the big name in the show. She rarely got any time off, so when she said she was coming to see me, I thought, *She must be interested a little? Even though I've messed her around a bit …*

We met a few times in London and then went out for dinner and started kissing, nothing more. We ended up spending the odd weekend together and had a great time. The problem was, I didn't want to ruin it. I still wasn't ready to commit to Jodi – not just anyone, *Jodi*. I wanted it to be perfect. I felt in my bones that this was the person I should be with for the rest of my life and I couldn't afford to risk messing that up. So, eventually I apologized and said it wasn't the right time. Understandably, Jodi didn't see why I was saying that, but I kinda cooled things off for a while.

We didn't really speak for the next few months, then in April I was at the Soccer 6 celebrity football tournament and Jodi was there. Nicky came into the changing room and told me. I started asking him, 'What does she look like? Is she OK?' I'd always be asking these questions, even though I wasn't with her, and if I heard she had a boyfriend I'd be raging jealous, even though I'd no right to be!

I saw her at the tournament and we chatted and she was quite blasé, not stand-offish at all, though after the way things had gone before Christmas, she had every right to be. This was all because of me – deep inside, I knew Jodi was for me, but I wanted it to be perfect when we finally did get together. I didn't want to rush it and make mistakes, break up, make up, all that.

She was still in *Hollyoaks*, still on all these magazine covers, and it was a constant reminder. I'd see these photos and interviews and think, *Oh no! I wonder if I've messed it up?*

About two months later we were on the Westlife *Greatest Hits* tour in Manchester. I'd been texting Jodi and had asked her to come down to the show. She had, and security had gone to fetch her and show her through to the dressing room.

When she walked in that night, it was WOW! Just like the first time I saw her all over again.

I look back now and think when I saw her at Party in the Park, it was probably love at first sight, then that night in Manchester, it was all those same feelings again. It was one of those moments in your life you'll never forget. She was 19 now and I was 23. When she walked in I was gobsmacked, knocked off my feet, literally. I thought to myself there and then, *This is it, she's the one. There's no way I can mess this up again.*

I was a different person that night with Jodi – she'd never seen me so interested. I was excited to be with her, listening to her every word. I definitely gave her the vibe that I wanted us to happen. We'd both been in relationships, but stayed in touch and now it seemed it was time for us to get together finally.

That night I told her how I felt. I said I knew I'd messed her around for those years. I explained everything that had gone on in my head and said I wanted to be with her. We kissed and talked and that was that. The next day I phoned her and said, 'I want you to be my girlfriend. This isn't just messing again.' She was reluctant to say yes straight away. She was a lot more grown up now and didn't want to get hurt. She finally did say yes, though, and we've been together ever since.

Six weeks later, we went on our first holiday together to Barbados. I'd been trying to tell her I loved her for about two weeks and I had grand plans how I'd do it on holiday, walking under the stars on the beach and all that. As it turned out, we were splashing around in the sea one day, messing around, having fun, when I suddenly stopped, held her close to me and told her I loved her. It was a very serious moment and she said she loved me too. We hugged and kissed and it was very special. The rest of the holiday was just like a fairytale – scuba diving, playing golf, walking, chatting, we did everything together.

Back at home, her part in *Hollyoaks* and my career in Westlife meant it was quite hard to see each other sometimes. She'd come down to London and I'd get up to Liverpool whenever I could. Then she decided she wanted to leave *Hollyoaks* and move on with her career and, with that, came down to London. I was delighted that she'd be so near!

We saw each other a lot more straight away, our relationship became more serious and then we moved in together. Then we got our dog Prince! I'd never had a dog and we'd talked about getting one, but I was worried that with our respective careers, it would be a big commitment. Our lifestyles are very busy and fast. Then one time I went surfing for a week, came back and there was Prince! I fell in love with him straight away, he's our little boy, and so now we have our family.

I started to think about asking Jodi to marry me. I'd always planned to go back to Barbados and ask her on the same stretch of beach and sea where we first said we loved each other, but I knew that if I did that, I'd just want to jump straight on a plane and tell all my family and friends and have a party! So at Christmas 2007, I made my plans. The day before, I asked Jodi's father for his permission and he said he was delighted. The next morning, we were opening our presents with Jodi's parents there. I gave her a stylish designer bag, but said, 'There is another present, but I'm still waiting for it to arrive.' Everyone except me and Jodi's father was very mystified! Then I went off hoovering and cleaning, and Jodi was like, 'What are you doing?!' I just wanted it all to be perfect.

What I was waiting for was for Jodi's sister and niece and nephew to arrive so I could ask her when we were all together. When they came for Christmas dinner, Jodi's father organized them all to head towards the kitchen and then I took Jodi's hand, told her to stand in front of the tree and close her eyes.

I had the ring in a box and went down on one knee and asked her to marry me. She threw her arms around me and hugged me tight and I said, 'You've got to say yes now!' She did and we hugged and kissed and everyone was so pleased. She'd not even looked at the ring! It was a very special moment of happiness. I got straight on the phone to Ireland and told everyone and it was brilliant, a lovely time. We've since been travelling around trying to find the perfect venue, because we both love the beach and the sea and want quite an earthy wedding.

Jodi understands my job in Westlife so well, having been in a band herself. Sometimes when I come home after we've had one of our heated band meetings, she talks to me about it and listens and it's brilliant. The boys get on great with her, too, which is fantastic. She is a rock and seems able to take me away from it all and remind me when I'm stressed that what I have is amazing and I should always treat it with respect.

I can't wait to be Jodi's husband, for her to be my wife and to have children and an amazing family life together. Jodi is incredible. There will never be anyone else. I am really lucky to have her in my life.

I started going out with Jodi in the same year I started my other love in life – surfing. In 2003, I was out playing golf with my dad in Strandhill, which has a mountain-top course overlooking the sea. We were teeing off and as I stood there, I looked down and noticed about 30 guys surfing out on the water. I'd always been a bit of a beach bum but I'd never actually surfed. For some reason, I suddenly wanted to give it a shot, so I came off the golf course with my dad and went straight down to the surf shop, spoke to the guy in charge, Tom Hickey, and said I'd like to try surfing. He said he could arrange a lesson, when would I like to go out? 'Er, we could go now?'

That was it and it's been fantastic ever since. I started off spending two hours falling off my board but, like everyone, I kept at it and now I absolutely love it. Part of the appeal is that when you go out in the ocean, you're in a different world and no one can get hold of you. When I'm surfing, no one can ring me on my phone, no one can call out to me to go somewhere, no one can come up to me. That's pure luxury. I'll often come off the surf and I'll have about 20 missed calls and 10 texts, but people know I surf now and it's cool. It's proper downtime for the brain.

It's important to have that release from the life in Westlife – in fact, it makes you better at being in the band because you get a chance to regroup and recharge. Shane loves his golf …

… and I've got my horses too, *says Shane*. I've got about 60 now and I absolutely love looking after them and being around them. Again, that's a complete distraction from the madness that is Westlife. It's a great release …

… and Nicky's mad into football, *continues Kian*. Mark … well, Mark loves his music! He has a love of all things creative: music, theatre, photography, art, he lives and breathes it.

Jodi says that when I go back to Sligo, I just live the lifestyle of a surfer. I do, she's right, and I just forget about everything to do with Westlife for a while. I'm still phoning round, speaking to the boys and Louis, but I just kick back from it enough to relax. Plus, my surf mates treat me like another surfer, not someone in a big band. I get treated like any other surfer. They've been to a few shows and said,

'Wow, it's weird seeing you up on stage in front of 10,000 people, doing all that!' At first, for quite a while, a few of them thought I was what surfers call a 'kook', a wannabe surfer, turning up in my jeep with all the gear, but they know now I'm really into it as a lifestyle. I go away on trips with my big surf buddies, Allan, Ken, Pete, Gary, Aaron; surfing is a big part of my life and every chance we get we go surfing. Even my friend Jason joined us as a photographer on a surf trip to Morocco.

Surfing has changed me, for the better, I think. Certainly as I've gone through my twenties, I've made better decisions just by being older and a bit wiser, but surfing helps too. The person talking here now is not the same person four or five years ago. I definitely think I've changed. For example, surfing stops you going clubbing – when we were in Sligo we used to always go out a lot, but I'd never go clubbing there now. I might go for a few pints in the local pub, but you usually surf early, and if you've got to be up at 6 a.m., you don't want to be out drinking till the small hours. It's the completely flip lifestyle to the late shifts you do in a band. When I went to Morocco with my surf mates in 2008, we were in bed at 10 p.m. every night, getting sleep ahead of trying to catch as many waves as we could early the next morning.

Surfing is proper chalk and cheese compared to Westlife, and I love it for that.

Nicky Kian Shane MARK xx

CHAPTER TWENTY-THREE

STAGE

After the success of the previous covers album, *explains Shane,* the record label wanted to do *The Love Album 2*, and they had even collated some really clever, interesting cover ideas. You can understand that too – they're a business, the previous project had done very well and they're there to make money, they're not a charity. But we weren't interested. This discussion about covers has, as you now know, been a constant feature of Westlife and we just wanted to put out an original record next.

For some reason, we are perceived by many people as a covers band even to this day, *says Kian.* I actually think that there's more concern about this within the band than there is anywhere else – it's not an issue with the fans, or Louis, or the record label. It's fair to say, though, that people forget we've had an awful lot of big hits with songs that are original. I think we get too much stick for this covers thing. There you go.

Once again, though, the discussion cropped up with regard to the opening single for the ninth studio album, which was to be called *Back Home*. The label wanted to release 'Home', a song co-written by Michael Bublé. We argued that it was too widely known already.

As Shane has mentioned, Nicky was especially keen on the track 'Already There', particularly with his twins having so recently arrived. Yet even that is a cover, albeit a lesser-known one. We'd been getting amazing reactions to that song when we performed it live but we decided, as a band, against it being a single, because it was a cover. We had had the same feelings about 'The Rose' and, probably most of all, 'Mandy'.

Now, 'Home' was another big hit, so in one sense the record label was right.

However, the song is a watershed track for Westlife, because we've said that we don't want to do any more covers. We are after world-class original songs.

The second single from the album, called 'Us against the World', is a good example of that – a great tune, some minor chords, a real edge to it.

I thought 'Us against the World' was such a great song, a bit cool, *says Kian,* but Sonny and Simon didn't really like it at all. They said they'd listened to 20 seconds of the demo and gone, 'Nah.' We were like, 'No! Listen to it again, because it is a grower.' To be fair, they changed their minds and Sonny was big enough to call back and say, 'Sorry, lads, this is a massive record.' But when it only went in at number 8, it kind of felt like egg on our faces. We'd never had a single out of the Top Five in the first week. Maybe it happened because the album was already out and that song was on there, I don't know. So that discussion about song choice is still ongoing – always has been, always will be!

We were very pleased with the album, mind. It hit number 1 and went on to sell around that magic million mark in the UK.

*   *   *

I think the shows after *Back Home*, in the spring and early summer of 2008, have been our best tour *ever*. Perhaps if I take you backstage with us for a moment, *says Shane*, to see what happens before a Westlife show and what leads up to the tour itself, you'll see how much we want to make it perfect every time.

First, we have probably seven or eight meetings with Steve Levitt – our production manager since the start – about what we want to do and he comes back with all the logistics, the costs, the pitfalls, all that. Then we start rehearsing six days a week with Priscilla, our choreographer, who Kian mentioned was so key for that first tour after Brian left. Then we start working six days a week with the actual musicians and try to get a vibe with them – what they enjoy, what fits in with the set, all those sort of ideas. We're not natural dancers so we have to be taught the steps really slowly, but once we get it, we're able to nail it. By this point, we're starting to fine-tune actual routines, moves, specific areas of the show. Then there are six days of what is called production rehearsal, and that's where all the major stuff happens – we go into what's basically an aircraft hangar and they set up the full stage that we will be performing on. So everything we have learned in a rehearsal studio in front of mirrors is now practised on the actual stage.

That takes about three to five days of long, hard hours. It's really tough work. But then by the end of it, we've probably run the show through completely three or four times, with dress rehearsals, too, and then we're ready to go.

The actual day of the show, *explains Nicky*, we'll probably get up mid-to-late morning, especially if there was a gig the night before – after which you usually can't sleep for a while! We get the tour bus to the show around about 4 or 5 p.m., depending on how far the venue is from the hotel. The bus drives us right up to the rear of the venue and we walk through, straight into catering. This is where all the crew, our backing singers, musicians and the band themselves eat before the show. It's a great chance to get to know any new faces too, having a meal and a chat.

Then, it's off to our dressing rooms, *continues Kian*. We all have our own ways of getting ready for a show. We all have individual dressing rooms now, which at first I was dead set against, I still wanted it to be the gang. But our circumstances have changed now, the children are here, and it has to evolve.

Mark likes to have his own space, so before he goes on stage, he'll go into his dressing room and have a few minutes to himself. I'll be out and about, chatting with people. I like to be around people, getting a buzz. The other two boys are usually with their wives and kids. I guess we each get ready in our own way. With the dressing rooms and the two tour buses, I was just worried the gang was splintering. It wasn't, it was just changing shape.

Show time comes and we head off to backstage, *explains Mark*. We have a cloth tent for the wardrobe, where all our costumes are hung up ready for the show. We'll already have the first costume of the show on by this point. Then the show starts and we head up the steps to the stage.

The costume changes in each set are done while the band is playing instrumentals or the girls are singing. We really have to rush – charge down the steps, straight into the wardrobe area, costume off, new costume on, make sure you are all zipped up and run out again. Our microphones are kept on a small table, on a towel, next to wardrobe, and we grab them as we run out and back up the steps!

Touring and playing live is what we love best, *says Shane*, and, for me anyway, what I was born to do. Being on stage is our favourite part of Westlife.

It keeps you fit as well! You always lose weight on tour because it's pure cardio five or six nights a week once you are up on that stage. We do strive to keep in shape and with so much attention on your appearance, you need to. A lot of my mates are in good shape. One of them, Brig, who I've known since I was four years old, is married to the gym. His body looks like Bruce Lee's. One day he looked at me and said, 'Would you not want to go to the gym?'

'What do you mean, Brig?'

'Well, listen, you're paid a lot of money to look well and, to be honest with you, you don't. You look alright, like, you're getting away with it, but you're not like you were five years ago.'

That's what friends are for!

Every time I saw him for a while, he'd say, 'Aye, you're getting away with it, but you're in Westlife, you need to cop on!'

Eventually it kind of sunk in – I should be going to the gym and I should be looking my best – and so I started training and working out. I started being able to wear a tight T-shirt and not be embarrassed and, with some of the costumes on stage, I felt much more confident and happier. I'm not exactly Bruce Lee now, but at least I can see Brig without getting the piss ripped out of me. I'm getting there. Brig reckons I'm about 60 per cent of the way there.

We all react differently to being on that stage, *reveals Mark*. When I'm standing on the stage itself, looking out at the thousands of people, I find that if I think too much about how many people are actually at the show, it can mess with my head. I sometimes have to cut off from thinking about it all, otherwise it's too much. For example, if I think a mum has brought three of her kids and maybe her friend to see our show, if you add up the tickets, the petrol, all the bits and pieces on that night out, she's probably spent over £200. She might have had to work a week for that. That's amazing, isn't it?

The problem is, if I stood there and thought that, I'd feel under too much pressure and I don't think I'd perform at my best, because I'd want my performance to be incredible in order to do justice to that money spent and effort made, and that'd make me too anxious.

When someone tells me they like my voice, it really does mean a lot to me. My voice drives me crazy though, as much as I love it! Sometimes I never want to sing again, it frustrates me. I see writers ripping up pages of words in anger and sometimes I feel like that with my voice. I might be on stage in front of thousands, but if I sing something I'm not happy with, I pull my mouth away from the mic and literally grimace at myself. It's that extreme – you love something so much you want it to always be perfect. When it isn't, it cuts me to the core. I never want to sing again, but that's only because I love it so much.

So, when I am standing in front of 20,000 people or whatever, I want to please them and I want to be pleased myself. I'm pressured on both counts!

We do multiple shows in most cities – and it's just too heavy to think about the money and the effort and the energy people are spending coming to see us! As a result, I don't ever go off and day-dream. I'm very much in the moment of the gig constantly.

I tend to try to disassociate myself from those numbers, I'll be backstage beforehand, phoning friends, chatting away, trying not to think about it basically. Sometimes I wonder if people see this and think I'm blasé or unappreciative, but I'm absolutely not, I guess it's just my coping mechanism.

We never go on stage without giving it everything, *says Shane*. There's always a first impression, there could be someone in the audience who didn't like Westlife for a long time and they said, 'I'll go and see what they're like,' and if they see a brilliant show, then we've made a new fan. Sometimes I might be very tired, but for some reason when I get on that stage, something happens, the voice comes from somewhere and I just do it! And it's hard not to enjoy it.

Then, after the show, it's back into the tour bus quite soon after we walk offstage, and back to the hotel or down the motorway to the next venue. So that's what it's like to be backstage at a Westlife concert.

There have been quite a few big changes on our recent tours, *says Kian*. Most obviously, Shane had his little Nicole and then, in 2007, Nicky's twins arrived. Deciding to take two tour buses on the road in 2007 was a big issue with me, you know. At first, I hated it. I said, 'Why are we doing this? No way, no way do we need two tour buses. There are four of us and those tour buses hold 18 people, why do we need two tour buses?' It was the same when we moved into individual dressing rooms – as I mentioned, I like the gang mentality.

However, our lives aren't the same as when we were five and then four lads roaming the world's stages. Shane and Nicky have children, Mark has Kevin and I have Jodi. The parents like to bring their kids on the road and it simply isn't realistic to think you can do all that in one tour bus. There's all the kids' stuff, they need quiet time to sleep and feed, and they have to get up at seven o'clock every morning, so it's essential to have more than one bus. I don't know what it's like to leave a kid at home for weeks, I can only imagine.

Louis understands that new dynamic totally as well, so it's a strong, strong team. Like me, he has changed his ways too an awful lot. He was very much an old-school boy band manager to begin with – no girlfriends in the press, no babies, no this, no that. Five available guys on the TV and in the magazines for the girls, good pop songs, good looks, that's how boy bands work. Now he is very happy for the bands he looks after to live their lives – just look at the amazing way he reacted to Mark's situation.

The boys all shared in my joy at finding Kevin, *says Mark*, and having someone special in my life. And when their babies arrived, I shared that joy too, as did Kian. Obviously, Nicky and Shane have the most direct joy at having their kids, but I'm so close to them as people that their children bring me genuine joy as well. Plus, as their friend, I enjoyed seeing them become parents and have the experience. When the little ones are around – as they often are on tour nowadays – then there is an extra slice of happiness in the Westlife camp.

It is different when you have to bring your kids with you, *says Shane*, and that's cool, because that's the way we are as people. We are like a family on the road – all the boys love all the kids and we all help each other out when we can. Kian and Mark have both got dogs now, too. It's all cool, like!

I think the boys are just great at supporting me and Nicky and our families. They understand our scenario and are there for support when I need help. Even if it's carrying a bag, one of them is always there. 'Do you want a hand? Are you alright?' To Nicole, Kian and Mark are uncles that she sees six days a week.

Westlife on tour has slowly just become a massive family on the road. We all understand we have very different styles of relationships that all need to be looked after and cherished.

*　　*　　*

It's been a long time since my teenage years of playing in rock bands like Skrod and Pyromania, *reminisces Kian*. Over the years, I've told plenty of journalists and many fans about those bands. It's been funny mentioning them. I still love rock music. Ever since our first few tours, I've been trying to slip a rock song into the set, but as you can imagine that's not easy with Westlife! I've mainly focused my rock hangover towards 'When You're Looking Like That', asking the guitarist to beef up his sound and use more distortion, but it's never really happened.

Anyway, for our March 2008 dates around the UK, I sat our musical director, Gary Wallace, down and said, 'We've got to put some heavy metal into the song, I've waited long enough!'

In rehearsals the guitarist, Pete, was making a fine effort, but it still wasn't distorted enough. So, oddly, I went and played him 'Sad But True' by Metallica to show him what I was after. 'I don't want that tinny distortion sound, Pete, I want it sounding fucking *rough*!'

'I've got a Gibson Flying V guitar, Kian ...'

'That's yer man!'

At one of the two Manchester dates, Skrod came back to bite me on my heavy-metal arse, though. I do the second verse of 'When You're Looking Like That', so while the other three are standing there, I run to one end of the stage, then back to the middle and then on to the other end of the stage, singing the line 'She's all dressed up for glamour and rock and roll.' All of a sudden, out of nowhere, Mark ran up to me and at the top of his not inconsiderable voice, with his face looking exactly like Gene Simmons out of Kiss, he shouted, 'SKKRRROOOOOODDD!'

I nearly fell off the stage from laughing.

Turned out he and Shane had been doing it behind my back all tour.

Fuckers.

Well i just wanna
finish by saying once
again thank You
for making all our
dreams Come true

All my love...

KEEPING THE DREAM ALIVE

A s we're finishing this book, *says Shane*, we are starting
preparations for the biggest concert of our lives, on 1 June
2008 at Croke Park in Dublin. It's sold out to the rafters, 82,000
people.

When the idea was first mentioned – by Louis, who else? – not
all of us were certain about it. I mean, *82,000 people*. You've got to
be pretty confident of your fan base to take that on. If you sell 72,000
tickets – enough to fill the old Wembley Stadium – the papers would
be full of how you didn't sell it out. Kian was a little concerned, Nicky
thought we'd sell out but that it would take ages and I was with Louis
on it, I thought we'd do it. But it was a gamble.

All the tickets were gone in less than nine days.

The initial 56,000 tickets went on the first day.

It's absolutely insane that we are doing Croke Park, *says Mark*.
Sometimes when the lads are going on about it, I literally have to

leave the room because if I build myself up, it's too much to comprehend!

Croke Park to me is incomprehensible, *says Nicky*. I've been there a million times supporting the Dublin GAA team. Georgina's been going since she was a kid as well, so all that rolled into one, it's going to be huge, and what an after-show party it's going to be!

When I think about the day, I smile, *continues Shane*. It's a Bank Holiday weekend and it couldn't be more perfect. I know I'm going to be absolutely taken aback by the size of the crowd, transported back to all those years ago in Newcastle on our first-ever headline tour when I was literally breathless.

We've played big shows before, like the two nights at Lansdowne Road to 40,000 a night. But over 80,000, I can't imagine it ... Croke Park will be the pinnacle of our career so far, the biggest night of our lives without a doubt.

I remember when I was 14, *says Kian*, I went to Croke Park to see Sligo play in the All Ireland Gaelic semi-finals. I recall thinking, *Wow! Look at the size of the place!* So to even dream of playing a concert there is beyond my wildest imagination. I really don't know how I will feel until I am actually there on the day. I know I'll be nervous, but it's going to be the most amazing thing I've ever done in my entire life!

One of the reasons why the Croke Park show is so important is that from 1 July 2008 we are scheduled to take a year off. We need to leave the fans with an imprint of just how brilliant the show was so they can't wait for our next gig when we come back.

This year off has been quite a big decision in Westlife. Now in the context of many bands, probably the majority, a year off is no big deal. Plenty of big acts take years between albums. But in our ten-year career to date, we've released nine albums. So a year off is a big deal to us and to our fans.

At first, I was all against the year off. I was like, 'A year off, what am I going to do with myself?' But I came round to the idea and I certainly think it's needed. It will give us all a chance to look back on what we have done.

When it was first mentioned, I kinda grilled each member on their thoughts about it. Now we all agree it is a good idea, a chance to pause before the next phase of our career, to look back and savour what we have achieved, but more importantly, to find a batch of absolutely world-class songs for our next album.

And I know what the boys are like! We've got this year off and we'll all still see each other anyway. That's why we're still together, because our friendship isn't forced. That's what Louis loved way back in the day – we were friends. In our year off, I'll go for a game of golf with Shane, I'll probably call round to Mark's and jet-ski on the lake and I'll be up in Dublin and see Nicky for a pint.

And I know them too well because for sure we'll then start getting phonecalls between each other saying, 'Hey, have you heard this song? What do you think?' I know we will, we love the music too much.

It will be nice to have a quiet Christmas and for the first time in ten years switch the telly on and not worry about the single or promo or all that. I think that's only natural. We've got families and girl-friends and boyfriends to consider now, so balance is important – in fact it's vital.

But I'll still be on the phone to Louis every second week and I know that as January starts coming round, the boys will want to start hearing even more songs!

The year off will give us some balance and it will, without a doubt, benefit the band. I think it will mean Westlife will continue for another ten years.

*   *   *

When you weigh up all the pros and cons of being in Westlife, *says Shane*, there are a lot more pros. In fact there is fuck-all bad about being in Westlife! Everyone gets annoyed about something in their job, and so do we. But not that much. Given what some people do for a living, how can we say otherwise?

Going into this year off, I think we are more driven now than we've ever been. We've gone past the stage where one bad turn can implode the band overnight. We have so many plans for the future. We definitely want to cement ourselves as one of the biggest bands in the world, without a doubt. That's what drives us on.

We are very aware that in the pop world, it's always about the next album. We want every new Westlife album to be massive, to sell all around the world, to be number 1 in all the big territories. That's how we think. To do that, we need great songs. That's what we all want – the record company, Louis and certainly the band. We want the next Westlife album to be our biggest yet.

I definitely think we can get to our twentieth anniversary, without a doubt. *Honestly,* I don't think that's unlikely or unachievable, not at all. We will strive to do that and I see no reason why we won't be there in another ten years' time. I'd certainly love to be, because I'd be the happiest man alive to see my kids at a Westlife concert, old enough to bring all their friends and to know what the band has achieved.

What we've done over this first ten years has been just like a dream, but it's our reality now. We just want to keep that reality going and that will keep the dream alive.

I know the three boys more than my own brothers in a way, *points out Kian*. I've spent more time with them – ten years on the road – and sat in more rooms and had bigger debates, conversations, arguments, hugs, kisses, tears and pints than I've had with anyone else.

I want to be in this industry for the rest of my life, I love being in this band. Doing this book has given me goose pimples talking about what we have done this past ten years. And it's made me certain we can do all of that again.

This isn't over.

This is just half-time.

When you sign a record deal at such a young age, *muses Mark*, you immediately enter a totally different universe from the one you've grown up in. Coming from such an idyllic country life, that was especially the case for me. As you know, I put up a barrier to stop my life changing. But now it has changed beyond all recognition. And virtually all for the better, because what I know now is that I can have Westlife and all the crazy experiences that brings, but I can have my family and friends *too*. My fears about losing my Sligo life were unfounded. Sure, I can't be at home as much as would be ideal, but the swap is brilliant.

I think, actually, that I am now addicted to Westlife. I don't think people realize this about me because for some reason I come across a bit nonchalant about the whole thing and a bit laid back, but I think about Westlife more now than ever.

I *love* Westlife with a passion. Having said that, it is very important to keep a perspective on things. Westlife is a great pop band, we sing songs and entertain people and, to be fair, quite a few people seem to like what we do. However, as a band we are under no illusions. We're not saving lives; we're not operating on brains. It's a band, it's pop music and there are certain things that it could never compete with, like family, friends, love ... *happiness*.

Westlife means the absolute world to me and I wouldn't want that last comment to come across like I don't care about it, because I do care about it more than almost anything in the world. What we have been so fortunate to achieve in this mad ten years is a successful life in Westlife *and* happiness with our families and loved ones – what an amazing privilege.

I absolutely love being in Westlife. I chose to do this, very much so. I didn't do anything against my own will. Westlife has allowed me to live the most amazing life and experience the most incredible things for which I will always be grateful. I've learned so much and had the most incredible time of my life. Looking back now, I don't honestly think I'd change a thing.

We're the only four people who have stood on that stage for ten years, *says Nicky*, sung those songs, made those mistakes, had those hits, had the adrenaline rush, had that same homesickness, had that same argument with Louis, that same praise from Louis, the same frustrations with the label, had their blood pressure shoot up to 190, met those famous people, spoken to those fans, been on those flights and those tour buses, recorded those words, played those gigs and been that band.

Will there ever be a band that can outdo what Westlife has achieved?

I doubt it, but who knows?

Either way, we've achieved something special and I don't think it will be surpassed for a long time yet.

We don't want it to end.

Hopefully, now you've read this book, you'll feel like you've been up there on stage, in the tour bus and in the studio with us. It's been some trip.

PHOTOGRAPHIC CREDITS

Plate Section

p10 bottom © Julian Makey/Rex Features, p12 bottom left © Vasiliki Kassiou, p14 bottom © ITV/Rex Features, p15 middle © Brian Rasic/Rex Features, p19 top, left (with Bertie Ahern) and bottom two photographs © John Ryan, p20 top left and group family shot © John Ryan.

All other photographs supplied courtesy of Westlife

Text pages (page numbers relate to first usage)

pxiv © ITV/Rex Features, p16 © ITV/Rex Features, p44 © Jeremy Crane/Rex Features, p128 © Rex Features